WHEN YOUR
PROTECTORS
DIDN'T

healing from a past of broken pieces

ANDI BULL

I'm sorry you've been hurt.

I hope this helps you heal.

Is not this the kind of fasting I have chosen: to loose the
chains of injustice and untie the cords of the yoke,
to set the oppressed free and break every yoke?

Isaiah 58:6 NIV

To Ben and Marge, for listening

To Larry Titus, for believing

To my people, for praying

To Ted and Zoe, forever

TABLE OF CONTENTS

PART THREE

Growing from Your Story

PART FOUR

Find Meaning in Your Story

YOU MATTER TO GOD

I sat by my father's bedside, his frail hand in mine.

"Are you cold?"

"No."

Silence fell between us. I could hear the hushed voices of people in the nearby kitchen, the sound of dishes being gently put away—life moving on despite sorrow. Looking at Dad lying there, so weak and diminished, I thought of the man he'd been before leukemia ravaged his body. Tall, powerful, filled with purpose, always busy, and highly influential in his position as the pastor of a renowned church. As a child, I'd feared yet longed for him. In adulthood, I'd lived to please him—a complicated man.

Dad's eyes searched mine. What was he looking for?

He drew a breath and said quietly, "I asked God to take me to be with Him while you were here this week. When He didn't, I knew it was because He wanted me to say something to you before I go."

I looked up at my husband Ted, who stood nearby, then back to my dad. My world stood still. A quietness entered the room that I'd not experienced before or since. My awareness heightened, I noticed everything: the cream-colored rails of the hospice bed, the IV fluid delivering much-needed pain medication, the faint hum of his blood pressure cuff, and his eyes, still so piercingly blue. He shifted in his bed, drawing strength.

"I'm sorry I abused you."

Boom. My heart pounded in my chest like a cannon. But he wasn't done.

"My mom, your Gran, used to beat me, and that's why I used the belt on you." He looked down for a moment before continuing, "I guess the saying is true: 'abused people abuse people.'"

Years, literal years in therapy, had not prepared me for this moment. Where were my words—all the things I'd longed to say?

How his devotion to the church, but neglect of our family, left me unprotected from Mom's abuse and others who abused me.

How his rage became my norm, a broken barometer by which to choose one broken relationship after another.

How I transferred my inability to please him onto God, spending years trying to earn His love.

All those words failed.

Instead, I discovered something incredible. When the apology I'd longed for came, I no longer desired it. I had taken back my story ages ago, rewritten my script, chosen forgiveness over bitterness, and found my way back to a loving God. My dad's apology could never undo the awful wrongs of my childhood and restore all that had been stolen from me. Only God could restore me, and He had done that—piece by piece.

Although well-meant, I realized this moment was more for Dad than for me. It was as though I'd been offered a lump of coal while sitting on a heap of hard-earned diamonds I'd dug from the wreckage of my past.

I didn't need the coal.

While his past may have defined his actions, the generational cycle of abuse had been broken by me. I had learned he was wrong—very wrong. Abused people do not have to abuse people. That's when the words flowed.

"Daddy, you don't need my forgiveness. I forgave you a long time ago. You go to be with Jesus, and let's put a comma here."

"Can I hug you?" he asked.

I leaned in, and he clung to me. It was the hug I'd yearned for as a child. The type of hug where your body releases all tension, and you finally breathe, knowing that someone bigger than you is there to protect you. Where you feel as though they have all the time in the world just for you—no church service to run to, no person in crisis calling to interrupt, and no situation worth displacing your importance.

Sorrow overwhelmed me for both of us, for the apologies that came too late in life, and for the relationship we could have had but never did. We'd both been robbed, but I believe he most of all. I had the rest of my life to celebrate my healing; he'd only had a moment.

———————

I don't know your story, but I wonder if you've had a similarly painful journey. I wish we could sit together and talk about it over a comforting cup of coffee, if only to offer you a safe place to share your hardships and assure you that you are not the problem. As most survivors can attest, we often feel to blame for childhood trauma, falsely believing if we hadn't been so "difficult to love," things could have been different.

Ideally, parents provide unconditional love and protection. They're available when their children come home from school and need loving arms to fall into after a hard day, to wipe away tears, bandage scraped knees, and prepare their favorite snacks.

Even though they make mistakes, these parents exemplify grace through the art of sincere apology. Discipline is understood as a form of nurture, enabling kids to grow into resilient adults who are prepared for the world's challenges. When the child comes to learn about their good, heavenly Father, the leap in logic is simple: if Mom and Dad are loving, God must be, too. With this understanding, they feel invincible.

When parents abuse their children or fail to protect them, children conclude that God must have the same nature. They may withdraw from Him out of fear or spend years trying to earn His love. Rather than feeling invincible, they wish they were invisible.

Unfortunately, as in my case, I did not even realize I projected my parents' brokenness onto God. As a result, I was afraid to get close to Him. You may have experienced this, also.

Recently, our family adopted a puppy. Sweet Koa came to us from a rough situation, and understandably, it took her a while to feel safe. However, over time, with love, patience, and treats, she let go of all her fear. Now, she jumps onto our laps whenever we call her name. Several times a day, a family member will say, "Who's a good doggy? Is it Koa? Yes, it is. Does Koa want a snuggle?" And we are rewarded with lots of happy tail wags.

Not unlike my sweet pet, when people are abused, it takes a while for us to trust again. Learning that God is not like those people who hurt you will take time. But God is patient and kind. He will work with you as long as necessary to restore His loving image to you and heal your broken heart.

When my sister and I were little, we loved going into the hall of mirrors at carnivals. We would run from one mirror to the next, playfully pushing each other aside to see our heads shrink to the size of peas and our bodies grow to the size of baby elephants. Distorted images are funny when you're young, but they can be deadly as you grow older. To name a few:

- If your parents disapproved of you, you may become a people pleaser.
- If your trust was repeatedly violated, you may fear intimacy.
- If you have experienced abuse, you may choose abusive partners.
- If you have been gaslighted, you fear that you are losing your mind.

These are just a few potential outcomes of a broken past, and healing from them requires time and effort. We need to be gentle with ourselves as we identify and untangle the lies we believe about ourselves and God.

———————

As a young girl, I read a book by Dr. James Dobson about the difficult things we experience during adolescence. Until that moment, I had not realized other teens struggled with the same things I did, and I felt comfort in knowing I wasn't alone.

In the same way, I hope my story brings comfort and support to you. Enduring trauma is difficult enough, with all its dreaded byproducts like anxiety, fear, inferiority, defensiveness, sadness, and anger. Nobody should have to walk this journey through life alone.

Thankfully, many people walked alongside me during my healing, some through licensed professional counseling, and others through mentorship. Those close to me have also benefited from medication and other resources available within the medical community.

My greatest help, however, came from my spiritual reconnection to God, and that is what I offer in this book. As I unraveled my past and began to read the Bible through the perspective of a survivor, God healed me. I recognized myself in the people Jesus touched, such as the man who literally endured hell on Earth, as described in Luke 9. When Jesus delivered that man, He restored his mind.

He did the same for me.

Jesus told the man to share with everyone what God had done for him, and that is all I hope to do as well. Every lesson I learned lies within these pages. None of my words are written to fix you, they are only meant to walk alongside you.

What I have not included are any details of the physical abuse I suffered at the hands of my parents, or when they, too distracted by their lives, failed to protect me from those who sexually violated me.

I want you to feel safe in these pages. You will only hear how I recovered and learn of the gentle paths God led me on to restore my broken soul.

My greatest hope is that by the time you finish reading this book, you will come to believe the truth about yourself, possibly for the first time.

You were made by God to be loved.

In grade school, our teacher taught us how to knit; we just had to provide the supplies. All the girls brought soft pink and brown yarn from home to make teddy bears. I guess our house had a yarn shortage on "pretty colors" because

I showed up with fluorescent orange, red, and green wool. While the other children patiently made little creatures with tight, tiny stitches and bright button eyes, I produced a disaster beyond compare.

Due to what also appeared to be a stuffing shortage at home, I used my old blue pajama bottoms. Nonetheless, when I finished my teddy, I happily held him up for a photo. Between me, with my ginormous front teeth, and him, with stuffing poking out of his lopsided body, I don't know who looked worse.

But darn it, if I wasn't proud of that bear.

Psalm 139:13 in the NIV states God "created my inmost being; [He] knit me together in my mother's womb." I pray that you had parents who cared for you and were proud of you, who wanted you. But if they did not, know this: your parents didn't knit you together; God did. And that makes you His creation.

I guess it's factual to say God also knew what you might have to survive when you came out. While I'm sure it broke His heart, He kept knitting. He knew that even if you emerged from your childhood stuffed full of leftovers and missing a few stitches, you would be His to hold for eternity.

Earlier, I shared my desire to sit together. The truth is, I have sat across from many people, over countless cups of coffee. I've seen their tears and heard painful stories of fathers, mothers, aunts, uncles, husbands, wives, and friends who hurt them or failed to protect them, leading to dire consequences for the victim. In turn, I've shared what God has shown me about Himself and the teachings He used to restore me. As fellow sojourners, we find healing together.

So, pour yourself a cup of joe, curl up in your favorite chair, and let's get to know each other—because just as these people matter to me, so do you.

And even better than that, you matter to God. And darn it, if He isn't proud of you.

PART ONE

VALUING YOUR STORY

CHAPTER 1

PERMISSION TO TELL YOUR STORY

When Healing Begins

I woke up late that first morning at my college friend's house in Galveston Island, Texas. It was Thanksgiving, and since I lived too far away to go home for the holiday, she'd invited me and some friends to stay with her parents instead.

Mama, as the family affectionately called her, had been waiting in the driveway for us to arrive, practically hopping from one foot to the other. The minute the car doors opened, she rushed to meet us with open arms. From her greeting, you would have thought I was her long-lost child, although we'd never met.

Their house was charming, though small, so I slept on the couch in the living room. Every inch of the home had multiple uses; this room was no exception. It also served as the laundry room, the machine tucked discreetly behind slatted doors. Before going to bed, I tossed a load in the wash and woke up to Mama standing nearby, trying to be quiet, a basket balanced on her hip filled with my neatly folded clothes.

"Hi," I said, yawning. "Wait a minute, did you finish my laundry?"

"Child," she replied in her delightful Southern drawl, "What have you been doing to your bras?" I couldn't help but laugh. She dangled the offensive object from her fingertips, its straps stretched like long rubber bands. I couldn't deny the truth. I'd practically murdered them. "Didn't anyone ever tell you these need to be hand-washed?"

Nope, no one ever had. The truth was I didn't talk about private things like bras at home, and until this moment, I never bothered to question why not. I pushed the thought from my mind—*Later, think about it later.*

Every night we laughed, ate, and talked till well past midnight. Every stray neighborhood kid wandered over to their home at some point that week, and there always seemed to be room for one more. The family spent hours in the kitchen, no tale off-limits. When my friend exposed our hooligan activities, like breaking into the football stadium to earn spirit points for our dorm, I waited for looks of disapproval–but there were none. Her folks laughed at our antics, chided us lovingly, or did both simultaneously.

An old wine jug covered in melted wax stood on the table where we talked and played Boggle. If someone picked the irresistible drips, they were lovingly scolded, "Now don't you pick that candle!" When the candle finished burning, Mama replaced it with another. It seemed silly to notice, but it impacted me. At my presentable home, an object like this would have been thrown in the trash, not revered as a table centerpiece.

But in Mama's home, everything was cozy and inviting. I felt loved and safe enough to talk about anything, even private things.

As we drove away, leftovers wrapped in to-go packages and a tearful Mama waving us off, all the girls fell asleep. I leaned my head against the window, watching the rain stream down the glass.

"You okay?" asked my friend, navigating the stormy roads.

"Yeah," I replied. "But can I ask you something?"

"Yes."

"Is it always like that at your home, or was that an act?"

"Nope. It's no act. I mean, it's quieter without all of us there," she laughed, "but that's us. Why do you ask?"

It seemed disloyal to share my upbringing with my friend—after all, I'd grown up with the mantra "don't talk, don't tell"—but seeing her home life struck me: *my home life had been different.* I gathered courage and told her about the times I was "disciplined," as the belt beatings were called. I told her about the terrible things that happened when my parents left me unprotected, passed from one abuser to the next. I told her about the fear I experienced living with so much volatility. When I finished, she spoke tenderly.

"Andi, you were abused."

"What?" I replied, shocked. "Isn't that how everyone lives?"

"No," she responded firmly. "They certainly do not."

I live in a beautiful agricultural valley in California, nestled among the surrounding mountains. The only downside is that we deal with poor air quality, which blocks the mountains from view. In winter, the cleansing rains come. After they pass through, and the pollen and smog are chased from the valley, the stunning Sierra Nevada Mountains are revealed. I will never forget the jaw-dropping moment I first saw the snow-capped peaks.

"Have those been there all along?" I asked a friend, who giggled at my disbelief.

This was how it felt to see the truth of my upbringing. Like suddenly seeing a mountain range I'd lived with for eight months and never noticed, I was shocked to discover I'd been surrounded by dysfunction my whole life.

Thank God I received validation from my loving friend the first time I shared my story. Because of her support, my healing journey began. It took a rainy day in Texas to wash away the illusion I'd grown up with. And once I saw, I could not unsee.

It isn't easy to have our eyes opened. We might feel betrayed, sad, hurt, angry, or anxious. Personally, as a truth-teller, I felt lied to. I could not believe what I'd endured under the guise of discipline.

In the Seventies, not many people talked openly about abuse, let alone the mental illness that often precipitated it. Issues such as depression, borderline personality disorder, suicidal tendencies, anxiety, narcissism, and passive-aggressive behaviors—to name a few—were largely unacknowledged in my day, and certainly not understood. We didn't have computers or the internet, and I had no idea what to do with my newfound awareness and sorrow. All I knew was, I'd endured a lot of unnecessary pain at home, a place where I should have felt the safest.

You've probably heard the saying, "Home is where the heart is." But I like to say, "Home is where the heart is formed," because, by the time we leave home, we have been shaped by our experiences within its walls, whether we like it or not.

You may be confused about your upbringing because you experienced good and bad times. For us, Dad worked hard and remained faithful to the church and my mother. Mom always put a meal on the table and, because money was tight, sewed our clothes. We experienced the normal range of activities: family dinners, movies, and vacations. Those times shaped me. But when I experienced the effects of severe dysfunction and neglect, those times shaped me, too. I developed imbalances.

———————

My friend and I took a road trip from Texas to Louisiana and spent the night in a very old, creepy house.

A long staircase, ascending alongside our sofa bed, led to a hobbit-sized locked door. By midnight, we'd convinced ourselves an intruder lay in wait behind the paneling. We barely slept, especially since an old-fashioned pendulum clock ticked noisily on the wall as it swung back and forth. In frustration, my friend yanked the clock down so we could sleep. The pendulum flung wildly out of sync and stopped ticking. We didn't know whether to laugh or cry.

In the morning, we wanted to fix the clock before leaving the creepy house. We hung it back up with much more care than it had been taken down, but it didn't work.

"I think we have to start it again," I suggested.

I recentered the brass pendulum, then tapped it gently to begin the swinging motion. Thankfully, it was ticking again by the time we left, spewing gravel into the air as we peeled out of the driveway.

Coming back to center after a traumatic childhood event is a lot like restarting that clock. The chaotic events and emotions surrounding abuse yank us out of the gentle rhythms of life. Some days we feel relieved, having gotten through with minimal damage, but then the next day, we may be ripped off the wall and put wildly out of sync. If Mom and Dad were angry, I bolted to my hiding place in the attic; if they were happy, I stuck around.

Like the clock, I needed to be recentered and rebalanced. At the time, though, I had no idea how.

———————

After graduating from college, I chose to confront my parents. It was *not* the place to begin my healing. They were outraged. The two of them rose, a united front, pointing everything back at me, as though I were to blame:

You were a difficult child; we were at our wits' end with you.
You'll ruin Daddy's ministry if you talk about this.
It was just a spanking.
How can you betray us like this?

They minimized and justified everything. Their reaction was so severe that I didn't gather the courage to talk to a therapist until I reached age 30. I didn't want to alienate or shame my family. I just wanted to discuss what happened and why. We had good and bad times, but two things I knew were true: I loved them. I was hurt by them.

While I can write about this now with no bitterness, it is *still* difficult:

To stand up for my narrative.
To posture myself in the powerful position of forgiveness.
To dismiss the voices in my head minimizing the trauma.

Recently, a devastating moral failure on behalf of a well-known pastor emerged. He had abused a minor and controlled her through fear and manipulation. The victim tried to advocate for herself but found little support. People refused to help her, afraid to confront the influential pastor. Years later, the truth finally came out. When she talked about her pain publicly, she spoke of being blamed for the abuse. As terrible as this is, it is all too common.

As if the mental and physical anguish survivors endure is not enough, by the time authorities believe them, any statute of limitations applied to the offender may be exceeded. Unsupported by the law or the community, victims find no .

closure, and are even told they are making things up. This is called gaslighting.

Justifications, denial, and recrimination all take a tremendous toll on your mind and body. But just because somebody tells you something did not happen does not mean they are right. Whether evil people get away with their insidious actions in this life or not, I know one thing for certain: one day, their deeds will be brought to light before God.

For now, be assured that when you share private things, you are sharing precious things. Do so with people you trust, because you deserve to be heard. This is your first step toward healing.

———————

Mom and I have a different ending to our story than Dad and I, as described in my chapter on forgiveness. But our road to a healthier end took some time. The way was messy and extremely difficult.

One terrible day, I stood alone, trembling on my driveway. I'd just had an upsetting conversation with Mom before she drove home. She told me one of my boundaries made *her* feel badly about *herself* and pressed me about why I continued to uphold it. After trying to explain my choice, using childhood events as evidence, I received the usual justifications. I longed for closure, yet once again, it eluded me.

That's when I sensed Jesus by my side—and heard Him speak to my heart.

I often sense Jesus's peaceful voice through Bible verses, song lyrics, or the beauty of nature. His words filter into my heart like a gentle thought that sounds like my voice but carries wisdom beyond me.

This time, His voice felt loving and firm. *You will never go through that again.* As I reflected upon His words, I felt

Him explain, *Every time you retell her the story, you have to relive the abuse.*

He was right. The trembling feeling in my body was precisely what I felt as a child. I was, indeed, reliving the abuse.

Right then, I buried any hope of receiving validation from my mother, as I'd received it from Jesus. If I kept pressing her to acknowledge what she had done, her frustration would rise, only to my detriment. My boundaries protected me and needed to remain firmly in place.

Instead, I took my pain to a safe community where I was believed, heard, and restored. I went to therapy.

My clock started ticking again.

The restoration process can be complex and lengthy. Mine took eight years of counseling interwoven with the guidance of a loving older couple who became like a father and mother to me. During this time, I cut off all ties with my family for two years. I needed the space to recover from their physical and verbal abuse, as well as the sexual abuse I endured from many others when Mom and Dad left me unprotected.

While difficult, I have never regretted my decision to prioritize my mental and emotional well-being.

In Matthew 7:6, Jesus said, "Do not give what is holy to the dogs; nor cast your pearls before swine, lest they trample them under their feet, and turn and tear you in pieces."

God wants us to honor our healing process as holy. The word "holy" means sacred and set apart. We do not give holy things to dogs. If our words are not heard, we must seek a different community who will listen. There are support groups, counselors, and advocates who can assist you and, if need be, accompany you to appropriate authorities.

We also do not throw our pearls to people who will trample them.

In my understanding, pearls represent something beautiful born through discomfort. Think of how they grow. When a grain of sand gets inside an oyster's shell, the oyster coats the irritant with mucus from its iridescent center. Remarkably, this produces something of value.

When people share their pain with me, I thank them for sharing their priceless pearls born through suffering. This is how I honor them. Just as a pearl takes time to develop, healing from the pain that produced it will also require time. It is of the utmost importance to place your story into the hands of those who will cherish it.

My family and I love the ocean. On one of our beach adventures, we found an isolated cove. Donning snorkels and flippers, we jumped into the water, listening to each other's muffled squeals when we spotted something fabulous.

As I let the current carry me, I saw something glinting on the ocean floor. Attracted, I dove down to find the most stunning shell, empty of an inhabitant, its two halves still connected. The outer shell was plain brown and unappealing, but inside, it had an iridescent center. Just then, rays of light pierced through the water, revealing luminous hues of pink and gold within the shell. It took my breath away.

Though you may not be able to see it at the moment, there is an equally breathtaking treasure within you. I pray that the light of heaven filters through your heart today, revealing the truth.

Your story shaped and produced something of infinite value—the story of you.

I pray that as you give yourself permission to share your pain, your healing will begin.

CHAPTER 2

ISN'T SHE LOVELY

Healing Your Worth

W e'd been on the runway for an hour. Angry passengers checked their watches and craned their necks into the aisle to check for movement from the flight attendants, but to no avail. The attendants remained seated and firmly strapped in. No word came from the captain, either. None of us knew the status of our situation. Outside the window, fluffy snow fell by the bucketload. I was grateful for the snow just a few short hours prior, as I skied my final run on Utah's mountains. But now? Not so much.

Finally, the captain spoke curtly, in no-nonsense fashion, like a parent giving bad news to their child and expecting no flak in return. "They're on their way to de-ice our plane. Thank you for your patience."

Half an hour later, the promised truck arrived and sprayed the plane like a giant carwash. Hope arose as the truck pulled away, but turned into renewed frustration when we learned it had run out of fluid and would return "shortly." Meanwhile, I took deep breaths to fight the growing pain in my body from an infection that required lots of bathroom breaks.

"Just get up and go to the bathroom," my husband said, as someone who is never afraid to advocate for himself.

"They told us not to move around the cabin," I whispered back, as someone who is always afraid to advocate for herself.

"Babe, you need to go." With that, he turned back to his movie. For him, the matter was settled. I couldn't argue, I did need to go. But:

- I didn't want to disturb anyone.
- I didn't want to draw attention to myself.
- I didn't want to get in trouble.

Can you relate?

———————

When I was young, a group of people hurt me, then bullied me into silence. I learned not to speak up for fear of punishment. I often wished I could be invisible. That's a challenging mental hurdle to break, to say the least.

Sitting on the plane, I considered my dilemma: suffer or get help?

I took a deep breath and reached up to press the call button. The flight attendant unstrapped and—*did she look angry?* — strode down the aisle toward my seat. I braced myself.

"You pressed your button?" she asked, arching her brow.

"I did, and can I please whisper something to you?"

"Yes," she replied, leaning down. I proceeded to tell her my predicament. I needn't have worried. Immediately, she snapped to attention.

"Follow me," said the flight attendant, now turned mother bear. She led me down the aisle to the restroom. Relief flooded over me as I stepped inside. When I came out, she waited with a cup of ice, cranberry juice, and water, and walked me back to my seat. I felt like the Queen of England. She stayed by my side, gently urging me to find care as soon as we landed.

Before I knew it, the entire mood of the plane lightened. Nearby passengers also engaged the attendant, who became quite chatty. She apologized for the inconvenience and expressed frustration at the lack of communication from the cockpit. People began talking to one another, asking in caring tones about missed connections, and so on.

In yet another turn of events, and, from what I could tell, without permission from the captain, she returned to the loudspeaker and announced that the crew would be providing water service while we waited. Everyone sighed with relief.

Soon after, we were on our way. I felt better; the people felt better; and the flight attendant felt better. And all because I'd pushed a button to politely ask for needed help.

Who needs your voice?

Was your response, "Other people?" That may seem like the natural conclusion of my plane story, and it isn't incorrect. Many people do need an advocate. However, I'd like to suggest an alternative answer.

You need your voice.

If your speaking up benefits others, that's wonderful. But others' well-being is not the focus during your healing. You have worth in this world. You are allowed to press the call button on your behalf.

There's a story in the Song of Solomon about a beloved and a dove.

The beloved calls to the dove to come away with him. He

tells her the long winter is over, spring has arrived, and doves everywhere are talking. But not this dove. She has silenced her voice and hidden away.

The beloved urges, "My dove in the clefts of the rock, in the hiding places on the mountainside, show me your face, let me hear your voice; for your voice is sweet, and your face is lovely" (Song of Solomon 2:14 NIV).

Doves are tentative creatures. At the first sign of trouble, they flit away. A mother dove nested in a plant outside our bedroom for weeks while she raised her family. If we merely cracked open the door to the adjoining patio, it startled her into flight. We decided not to use the patio.

Conversely, when doves are happy, they talk. A LOT. They almost cooed us to death that spring. By the time the babies flew the nest, *we* were exhausted! We prudently moved their breeding grounds away from our door when mating season ended.

"Let's just put this plant somewhere else," I told my husband, as he hastily helped me drag it away.

We don't know what had frightened the dove in the Scripture passage, but her demeanor is strikingly similar to someone who has encountered bullies in the past. She went to great lengths to disappear. The beloved, however, knew exactly where she was...

In a cleft. In a rock. In a hiding place. On the mountainside.

She may only be one dove among many, but she mattered to him, down to her precise location.

I know it's hard to feel your value after a lifetime of neglect. Although you may have felt unseen by your intended protectors, I assure you, you deserve to be seen and heard. God knows where you are hidden and why. He understands that you might be afraid to come out of hiding and face the past. You are not the first of His children to feel that way.

———————

Moses fled Egypt after he killed an Egyptian master for beating a Hebrew slave. He hid in the Midian wilderness, seven hundred miles from where his life began, and stayed there for forty years. Might as well have been...

In a cleft. In a rock. In a hiding place. On the mountainside.

Still, God knew where to find him and how to get his attention.

As you can imagine, after forty years in the wilderness, Moses had seen a lot. But when he saw a burning bush that would not incinerate, he went to investigate.

As he drew near, God spoke from the bush and told him to remove his shoes. An ordinary place had transfigured into a holy space. He then gave Moses an assignment far bigger than he would have ever chosen for himself: to rescue His people from bondage. Moses sought to inform God that He'd picked the wrong person.

"Who am I?" Moses asked.

But God didn't respond by defining *who Moses is*.

He revealed *who He is*: "I AM WHO I AM" (Exodus 3:14).

God's name is positive—more on this in a moment–He didn't say, "I am not..." His name is also in the present tense. Because even though He lives outside of time, He is eternally with us in each moment.

Moses, more than likely overwhelmed, still only saw his disqualifications. But where he saw flaws, God saw virtues, imperceptible to Moses. Everything Moses thought disqualified him, actually qualified him.

- Moses had humility.
- He identified more with the enslaved than the princes.
- He despised injustice.
- He knew the ways of Egypt.
- He knew the wilderness like the back of his hand.

True, Moses had to face his past. But this time would be different. Whereas he'd once fought his battles alone, he now had a powerful advocate by his side. God promised to go with him, to show him wonderful things.

On this healing journey, you are no longer alone. Not only will God fight for you, He will also fight *with* you, sending His Holy Spirit as a comforter. He will guide you to counselors, friends, and a supportive community. Together, you will discover something wonderful—that you are worth fighting for.

Just as God's name is positive, we too can define ourselves by who we are, rather than who we are not. This helps to give us the courage to face difficult things, such as our past or an uncertain future. Even John the Baptist defined himself by an "I am" statement. He said, "*I am* the voice of one crying in the wilderness" (John 1:23). Here are some of my affirmations.

In Christ:
I am unmoved by waves of doubt.
I am fruitful.
I am forgiven.
I am His eternally.
I am worthy of love.

We empower ourselves and others when we speak positively. Years ago, I stopped trying to correct people, or criticize them. I decided to be kind and encouraging, leaving the rest to Jesus. I now have more coffee dates than I have time for.

People are attracted to authentic messages of positivity and kindness. I didn't have many people who were kind to me in my childhood, but I remember everyone who was. They used their voice to bless me. Bless yourself daily, and then extend that blessing to others. The world has enough negativity in it. Let's be different.

Let's love people until they see Jesus.

Once we start believing good things about ourselves, we can begin to believe in God's purpose for our lives and how deeply He values us.

Dad and Mom had two completely different versions of my birth account. Despite our troubled history, Dad's was fantastic. He had come to the hospital from the church, wearing his black suit and clergy collar—a piece of white plastic popped into the collar of his shirt. At the time, ministers of all church denominations wore the same outfit.

He saw a nurse wheeling a baby to the collective nursery. On a hunch, he asked, "Nurse, whose baby is that?"

"Let me look at the tag, Father," she said, mistaking my dad for a priest. When she read my name, Dad said excitedly, "She's mine!" The nurse pursed her lips in disgust as if to say, "You dirty old priest."

Undeterred, Dad kept staring at me. At that exact moment, I opened my eyes. "The bluest eyes I'd ever seen," he recounted. It was a good story—the best. I had him tell it often.

Mom's version, on the other hand, wasn't so great. You would have thought she gave birth to something that belonged in the zoo. While I loved Dad's birth story better, Mom's made a greater impact on me.

For some reason, negative things we hear about ourselves can overshadow the positive. Getting rid of that thinking is hard.

It reminds me of the famous video of a sheep stuck in a ditch. A young man rescues it by pulling it out by its leg. No sooner has the sheep bounded away than it jumps back into the *same* ditch, stuck again. Letting go of old beliefs is like that. We can bounce out of one rut only to get trapped in another.

To avoid repetitive ruts, we can replace negative thoughts with positive ones. These days, if a thought wants to live in my head, it has to answer affirmatively to two questions:

1. Is it kind?
2. Is it true?

We may not initially believe the kind words we speak to ourselves, but one day we will—and that is a *great* day.

Sometimes, I still have hard days. When the pain of my past beats down like an unrelenting rainstorm, I tend to want to seek shelter in the rocks, like the dove who hid herself away.

On one of those days, as I pulled some sweats and socks from various drawers in my closet to prepare for taking my pups for a walk, I felt Jesus's familiar presence. I stopped what I was doing and closed my eyes. A thought fluttered into my heart.

I felt Him say, *I want to heal your mom's version of your birth story.*

He had my attention. I lifted my hands, waist high, with upturned palms. "What do you want to tell me?" I asked.

I want to share my thoughts about the day you were born.

Suddenly, the tune of Stevie Wonder's "Isn't She Lovely" filled my mind. I searched around on my phone for the song and listened with renewed interest.

Tears streamed down my face as I heard a father sing a

love song to his newborn child, declaring her lovely, wonderful—loved. If you did not know, Stevie Wonder was blind from birth. And yet he saw better than most, because he saw through the eyes of love. And in case you didn't know this either, the song title on the album cover does not end with a question mark. Stevie Wonder is not *asking* if anyone else thinks his daughter is lovely; he is *stating* she is.

God is your Father, and He loves you dearly. He is truthful and cannot lie. When He says your voice is sweet, He truly means it. When He calls you lovely, it is not a question but a statement. No matter what you've heard about yourself, this is your amazing new birth story—the best.

I pray that you allow God to tell it to you often.

PART TWO

REDEEMING
YOUR STORY

CHAPTER 3

LIMITLESS LOVE

Healing the Image of God

My friend Jennifer chased her seventeen-year-old son through the streets of a derelict beach town. He spotted her from a distance and sped off through the dark alleyways.

David lived the life of an addict. He'd rebounded in and out of rehab only to finally succumb to life on the streets, begging for drug money. There had been hopeful times when he'd come home to get clean, sober, and fed. But soon enough, he'd disappear, often for weeks. Despair filled his parents' hearts. When friends called to tell Jennifer they'd spotted David, giving his whereabouts, she'd jump in the car and bring him home again. On this occasion, rather than accepting her approach, he bolted. The police assured her they'd search for him, with nothing else to offer as consolation.

Time passed. Despite many search attempts, no trace of David was found. The torment of not knowing whether he was dead or alive consumed Jennifer, yet she remained steadfast in looking and praying. One day, the miraculous happened. Her phone rang from an unknown number. A voice said, "Momma. I'm on the boardwalk. I wanna come home."

When she found him, David was filthy. He smelled of urine, his clothes were soiled, and his hair matted to his face. He lay on a bench, barely able to lift his head. The stench, the feces-stained garments—none of it mattered to Jennifer. She did not hesitate a moment. This was her dear child, thought dead but alive. She threw her arms around him, pressing her cheek to his.

"It's okay," she whispered, gathering him to herself, "I've got you now."

People with broken hearts often struggle to comprehend such unconditional love. Crippling shame can drive us to dark places, internally and literally, where we act in ways contrary to the beloved child we are. I've been there; I know. Simply put, we do not believe we are worth the trouble. Somewhere along the way, our image of God broke, and with it, our image of self. Many believe that to get right with God, they need to get "cleaned up" first.

The truth is, when sinners met Jesus, their cleanliness was the last thing on their minds. The same people who wouldn't be caught dead going to synagogue—often, not even allowed in the doors—ate with Him and poured treasured oil on His feet. Prostitutes, tax collectors, adulterers, and drunks came as they were and loved Him. They were sin-sick; He was the doctor. Simple as that. What was it about Jesus that drew the broken but repelled the religious?

I believe it was His overwhelming compassion for their humanity. Isolating the unclean had reached new magnitudes by the time He arrived. While the law required one to purify themselves, the Jewish ruling parties, the Pharisees and Sadducees, added their own endless rules. Jesus called these traditions heavy yokes. He was angry that the priests, who were meant to connect people to God, made it impossible for people to reach Him.

Jesus came to re-represent God, so to speak, to a hurting people. He rebuked religious people who distorted the spirit of His Father's merciful heart. He touched the unclean, an unprecedented act, to heal them, restore their dignity, and reintegrate them into the community.

While studying for my master's degree, I rented a beautiful cottage in the hills of Southern California. On the day I met the landlord to sign the lease, I extended my hand to offer a welcoming shake. He quickly jerked back several steps. Confused, I asked a professor at my seminary about the encounter. He explained that according to my landlord's religion, he believed I could make him unclean if I touched him and happened to be menstruating.

I can assure you, one of us felt unclean that day, and it wasn't the landlord. I was ashamed by his look of dismay and that, in my innocence, I had nearly broken his rule of purity.

Shame is a crippling byproduct of feeling unclean due to the things that have happened to us. In turn, acting out of shame, we may try to normalize the experience by repeating it. It creates a vicious cycle, only interrupted by grace.

Before Jesus's arrival, neither sinners *nor* priests understood God's "crazy-about-you" love. And when they experienced it in the person of Jesus, it revolutionized their lives in different ways. Sinners abandoned their lifestyles to follow Him, attracted to His warmth as one is to a cozy fire on a frosty night. The religious leaders, on the other hand, plotted His death with indignation.

Nonetheless, Jesus persisted. His Father's image had been distorted, and He'd come to reflect it correctly. He told them a story—much like Jennifer's—of a relentlessly devoted parent. If He felt it worthy of telling, then I do, too.

A wealthy father had two sons. The youngest asked for his share of the inheritance while the father was still alive. He no longer desired a relationship with his father; he secured the money, and then cut ties.

The father did as the son asked. You may ask yourself why he gave in. Didn't he know his self-centered son would squander it? Probably. But here is our first insight into this unique father: He refused to control his son. He honored his free will and allowed him to make his own choices, however poor. He knew that freely given love must be freely reciprocated. So, he let him go.

The son took the money and spent the lot through reckless living. Soon, famine struck the land, and the wayward child became destitute. In what would have been considered an abomination to Jesus's Jewish audience, he could only find work amongst unclean animals as a pig farmer. Mercilessly, the employers refused to feed him, not even a single pod from a pig.

One day, at rock bottom, he finally decided he'd had enough. He considered how abundantly his father's servants were fed and decided to swallow his pride. He'd go home. On his way, he rehearsed his speech: "I am no longer worthy to be called your son. Make me like one of your hired servants" (Luke 15:19).

No longer worthy. I have lost my worth. I am worthless.

Have you ever felt worthless?

A friend grew up in an abusive household filled with shifting conditions and requirements. She fell into drugs and alcohol. At her lowest, she cried out to God and felt His forgiveness, but wrestled with embracing the peace of His unconditional love. One night, she had a dream where she died and went to heaven, but arrived as a flip-flop. She finally made it, but only as a shoe. We still laugh about it, and I occasionally tease her by calling her Flippy.

Nevertheless, the dream revealed her core belief: *I may eventually get to heaven, but I'll be on the lowest rung.* Like the son, she thought she could only please God as a servant, not fit to be adored as a child.

I have many friends who fear not quite making the cut. They go to the altar every Sunday to get re-saved, just in case. They do not understand that our incredible value *never* changes. God considered us worthy even when we were covered in the world's filth. He loved us even when we were sinners.

By sharing the wayward son's thoughts, Jesus revealed an all-too-common human misunderstanding: God's love is conditional. We believe that when we inevitably fail, we must grovel to regain His good graces. If you grew up with a parent who loved you conditionally, you may believe acceptance is based on performance. It is not.

The young man in the parable had a limited understanding of limitless love. Can you imagine his long, desperate walk home? I picture him in filthy clothes, occasionally stopping to catch his breath, hands on his knees, lips parched, practicing his speech.

Take me as a servant. Please. I don't deserve to be a son again.

But once a child, always a child. And the father waited. Only the Bible does justice to the story: "But when he was still a great way off, his father saw him and had compassion, and ran and fell on his neck and kissed him" (Luke 15:20).

Time and culture keep us from fully understanding the impact of these words on Jesus's Jewish audience. First, Middle Eastern men did not run, as it could put them at risk of shamefully exposing their undergarments. Second, his child was covered in the stench of pig manure, an unclean animal. The expectation would be for the father to scorn him, keep a distance, or, at the very least, demand he be cleansed and purified before approaching.

Not this father. He'd been actively scanning the horizons, aching for his long-lost child. Filled with compassion, he disregarded tradition and ran to embrace his son and kiss him, becoming unclean in the process. He did not care. Imagine the servants' mouths hanging open in astonishment as they watched the scene unfold. But they didn't get to stand around long. Soon, the orders flew:

Get the best robe. A ring. Shoes. Kill the calf I've been fattening up (was it for this occasion?).

The son's condition didn't matter, only that he had survived. The son's actions had done nothing to diminish his worth. He was loved. Period.

If you ever question how desperately and deeply Father God loves you, this story should dispel all doubt.

But there was another son. *He* hadn't left or squandered his inheritance or broken the father's heart. He'd been the go-to guy, running the father's affairs and never asking for a thing in return. He was so good that, according to his accounts, he'd never even broken a commandment. Ugh. Older siblings. Why are they so perfect?

One day, after diligently working in the fields, he heard the sound of a party. A servant told him the good news that his brother had returned. Rather than rejoicing, though, "He was angry and would not go in" (Luke 15:28).

Imagine the crowds gathered around Jesus, poised on the edge of their grassy seats to hear the reconciliation. Would the father side with the older brother in this topsy-turvy tale? Would he change his mind about forgiving the prodigal?

In another remarkable twist, the father did neither. Instead, he humbled himself again.

He went to his son and listened as the anger poured out. And then he pleaded, "Son, you are always with me, and all that I have is yours. It was right that we should make merry and be glad, for your brother was dead and is alive again, and was lost and is found" (Luke 15:31-32).

The story ends here, and the message is clear: Just as the younger son's actions did nothing to *diminish* his worth, the older son's did nothing to *increase* his value. They were both loved equally.

The father in Jesus's story only knew how to love his children. Compassionately, he fought to reconcile his family. Nothing stopped him, not:

- Pigs
- Filth
- Wild living and prostitution
- Self-righteousness
- Pride
- Scorn
- Sibling rivalry
- Anger

Jesus offered His audience a different image of God than they'd seen modeled for them. Our heavenly Father is loving, courageous, humble, forgiving, and unrelenting in the pursuit of His children. He is not mean, dictatorial, or punitive. He can be approached, again and again. All of His is ours for the taking.

If we fall into thinking that He is unforgiving or demands

performance, we will lose our way. We will either run off with the pigs or go through all the religious motions to please Him, scorning everyone who isn't trying as hard as we are. Neither of these will do.

When we run away, He searches the horizon. When we get angry, He pleads with us to see things through His eyes of grace.

If, today, you find yourself in the image of the older son, burned out from trying to be good enough, then *let go*. The price has been paid; the toll has been counted. You are free to embrace the Father, covered in the perfection of the Son of God.

And if you embody the younger son, on the run, living with pigs and covered in the world's filth, then *come home*. Return to Him. It will be okay; you are loved and forgiven. Lean in close and hear His heart. I can almost hear His words ...

It's okay, child, I've got you now.

CHAPTER 4

APPEASING UNAPPEASABLE PEOPLE

Healing the Message of Not Enough

A young man who is like a son to Ted and me told us a story from his teenage years. He grew up near a large outdoor concert venue in Colorado. The day before a show, crews placed bright orange construction cones along the roads to help attendees navigate the country roads more easily.

He and his friends had the not-so-brilliant idea to reroute the cones "just for fun." They waited until the workers left, then repositioned the cones in the direction of a random hill, creating a new path. They then hid behind some bushes to see what ensued.

Completely unaware they were heading in the wrong direction, concert attendees dutifully followed the new boundary lines, arriving at a dead-end hill far from the event. With no exit lane, a pile-up ensued. People honked and shouted at each other; then, sirens blared as police arrived and, incredulously, started handing out tickets. In the chaos, the kids got scared of potential repercussions and bolted home to hide. I couldn't help but laugh at his look of dismay as he retold the story and the disastrous conclusion.

As bad of an idea as it was, the story makes a good point: just because a path appears legitimate doesn't mean it should be followed.

As children, we dutifully traveled the paths established for us by grown-ups. It was what we did, even if the cones led up the wrong hill. When I displeased Mom, she recited a poem to me:

> *There was a little girl who had a little curl*
> *Right in the middle of her forehead.*
> *When she was good, she was very, very good*
> *And when she was bad, she was horrid.*

Desperate to prove I wasn't a horrid child, I became a people-pleaser. I traveled the perilous path often. And no matter how hard I tried, it always ended in the same way: she remained unhappy.

My attempts to earn my mother's approval or simply gain her attention were rebuffed or ignored. I felt like the woman in Mark's gospel who poured her precious oil on Jesus's head, only to have her gift called a waste. How could I have known then that nothing would ever be enough for Mom? She was a broken soul at the time; and I was not responsible for fixing her.

In trying to please Mom, I developed a codependent core belief: *I am okay if she is okay.* Since my well-being revolved around hers, I lived to make her happy. Because of the turbulence within her soul, I could never have understood the impossibility of such a task.

I remember the pristine beaches of Florida, with seemingly endless white sand stretching for miles into the distance. I'd lie on my towel after a swim, eyes closed, basking in the sun's warmth and the delightful sensation of salt prickling my skin as I dried off. I could hear the ocean waves crashing onto the shore and cheeky gulls calling to each other. Suddenly, out of nowhere, I'd feel a chill. The skies would darken, as thunder rumbled and a storm approached. Almost before I could scoop up my towel, rain would begin to pour in torrents. I'd run for shelter, shivering beneath a nearby tree. One minute, warm and cozy; the next, miserable. That's how quickly moods shifted in our home.

In adulthood, I inadvertently chose relationships with mercurial people, entering each with the same goal: to please them. I didn't realize I was trying to fix a core relationship gone wrong. True to form, none of my efforts were enough.

It's the old idiom about setting a cornerstone for a building correctly. If the cornerstone is not properly placed, the entire structure risks toppling. With my relationships resembling the Leaning Tower of Pisa, I recognized the need to examine my cornerstone. In so doing, I discovered the lie engraved upon it:

I am horrid and must prove I am not.

In every relationship, I started in deficit. No wonder I lived on a hamster wheel, wearing myself out trying to please others. My self-worth could no longer be determined by this lie or by people for whom nothing is ever enough.

In the Gospel of Matthew, Jesus tells the story of ten women waiting for the bridegroom to arrive at a wedding feast. Traditionally, in this culture, the bridegroom surprised the bride with his arrival—I don't think that would go over too well today. Nonetheless, guests were expected to be prepared for any possibility, including delay. The symbols of their preparation were lamps and oil.

Five arrived with lamps filled to the brim with oil, and extra, just in case things took longer than expected. This is a picture of a healthy person. They take their responsibilities seriously, prepare for unexpected outcomes, and do not expect others to cover for them. They understand that failing to do their part burdens others unnecessarily. They do their work, believing that the celebration will be worthwhile. Jesus calls them wise.

The other five women arrived with only one lamp. When the bridegroom took longer than expected, they ran out of oil. Instead of taking responsibility for their lack of preparation, they did what many emotionally unstable people do: they went to those who had prepared properly and demanded their oil. In other words, they assumed that others should solve a problem they had created. Jesus calls these women foolish. It is a picture of an *unhealthy person*:

- Demanding
- Entitled
- Expecting others to do the hard work

Here is the lesson. We are not responsible for the emotional well-being of others. While *we can* certainly support and love people, their inner empty places can only be filled by time spent with Jesus and the transformation He works in them. We are only responsible for the oil that fills our lamps.

When we focus on pleasing others, we feel compelled to

say yes to those who demand it. The wise women focused on the bridegroom. They said, "No, lest there should not be enough for us and you; but go rather to those who sell, and buy for yourselves" (Matthew 25:9).

With no alternative, the foolish women went to get more oil. Meanwhile, the bridegroom arrived, and the five wise women joined him at the feast. The foolish women returned too late—the doors had shut. At the story's end, Jesus, by intimation, commends the five young women for choosing *not* to share their oil.

We will miss the point if we make this a parable about sharing. It is a parable about priorities and wisdom. The five wise women aligned their priorities with the bridegroom, who represented Jesus. He wanted them to be prepared for His arrival. This meant there was a time to say yes and a time to say no.

In healing, we need to streamline our activities to give our journey the attention it deserves. People who are accustomed to you always saying yes may struggle with your new priorities.

That is okay. Let them struggle and adjust.

When I was eight years old, Jesus spoke to me in a profound encounter, saying, *I have called you to heal.* Later, He repeated the phrase but emphasized the word "you." I understood that even though I had been wounded, it did not exempt me from the hard work required to heal. I could not use my past as an excuse to stay broken in the present or to demand that others do the job for me. As hard as it was, I had to take charge of my journey.

This is wisdom: healing, growing, and giving to those in *genuine* need, while resisting the urge to please those who believe their happiness depends on you. We must follow the wise women's path and embrace the truth. We will never have enough for ourselves while healing if we continue to give in to the endless demands of unappeasable people.

There comes a time when we must draw a line around our values and say no to people. We have different conversations that reflect the wisdom of Jesus's story.

_____

Here are some thoughts you might consider based on the lessons in the parable:

- Recognize that you will not have enough resources for yourself and those with legitimate needs if you give them to unappeasable people.
- If you give your time to demanding people, you will not have enough time to prioritize Jesus's loving requests. Jesus never makes us feel guilty; He asks and invites.
- Your job is to fill your lamp; others fill theirs. Their unwillingness to prepare is not necessarily a call to action on your part.
- Oil is costly. I paid financially and emotionally for my healing, which took years. Others can also pay the price of preparation and hard work. This is their responsibility.
- Jesus tells us we are the light of the world. We must keep our lamps lit to contribute to God's kingdom.

_____

I am much happier when my little lamp is full, and I say yes from a place of abundance rather than deficit.

Too many times to count, I have asked God to get me out of commitments I made because I felt pressured to say yes when I wanted to say no. "Please let them cancel," I prayed. One day, God told me to be prepared with a "holy no," meaning to give Him authority over my yes or no before giving it to others. Tentatively, I began to say no when He asked me to.

Some people became upset. But hopefully my saying no prompted them to reevaluate their reasons for always saying yes, to address their overwhelmed lives. For me, it proved to be a powerful tool for identifying healthy friendships. Supportive friends graciously replied, "No problem," and even offered to help me. They are my friends to this day.

Saying no to demanding people isn't easy, at least not at first. But it get's easier with time. And then when you do say yes, from a place of inner security, rather than trying to earn approval, your acts of service become enjoyable.

———————

Earlier, I briefly mentioned the woman of the Bible with her precious jar of oil.

There are so many dynamics in this story. A grateful woman poured her costly perfume on her Savior's head, bathing Him with the fragrant oil. I can barely comprehend such an extravagant act of worship.

Despite her sincerity, the men standing about shamed her. They called her gift a waste—and thus called Jesus a waste—because they did not consider Him a worthy recipient of such extravagance. For them, even the Savior of the world was not worthy enough.

The world is full of people with impassable standards.

Note Jesus's words as He defended her: "Leave her alone. Why are you bothering her? She has done a beautiful thing for me" (Mark 14:6). Her gift was more than enough for Jesus, who called it "a beautiful thing." He promised she would be remembered wherever people told the gospel story. Remarkable.

Jesus considers every heartfelt thing we do significant, even giving something as simple as a cup of water. He happily receives our gifts of love, big or small.

———————

My daughter Zoe created one art project after another for me as a child. She glued beads with sticky fingers onto cardboard cutouts and proudly gave them to me. I cherish each one. Why? Because she is my beloved child, and every gift from her is a token of love that penetrates my heart. She doesn't have to earn my love; she will always have it.

We are God's beloved children. He does not wait for us to do enough or become enough to love us. We are born loved, and we stay loved. He will never speak condescendingly or criticize us. Knowing we can never fulfill the Law's demands, He took care of everything through Christ's death; we can do nothing to add to our salvation. We are enough in Christ.

Knowing this truth frees us to please God in response to His love, not to earn it.

I'm ready to dance into eternity with the beauty of this realization. In so doing, I replaced the lie on my cornerstone with the truth: I am beloved. And while I was at it, I rewrote my poem.

There was a little girl who had a little curl,
Right in the middle of her forehead.
And when she did well, she was very, very loved,
And when she tried and failed, she was loved just the same.

Well, it may not rhyme. But now it's finally true.

CHAPTER 5

THE IDOL OF MINISTRY

Healing Church Wounds

give you permission to exit all toxic relationships."

I looked at my husband to see if I'd heard our pastor correctly, as such advice is not preached in most pulpits on sleepy Sunday mornings. I'd heard it plenty of times in therapy. But never in church.

Ted nodded affirmatively. *Yep. He said it.* I hastily scribbled the words into my notebook and hugged it to my chest, almost afraid the advice would disappear. People need pastors to stand up for them in areas of mental health. Sadly, this is often not done.

As I pondered his words, I realized something. While I had worked hard to weed out toxic relationships by confronting my unhealthy motives—trying to appease unappeasable people—my longest toxic relationship had not been with a person. It had been with the church.

When the church doors opened, our family was there, dressed to the nines. It didn't matter if all hell broke loose the night before during some argument; we were required to attend with smiles glued to our faces, as if everything was great. You would have thought we were the perfect family.

After the sermon, Dad stood at the door, hugging everyone who desired. His robes were stained with tears and makeup from the crying women. He looked on them benevolently, filled with compassion. I have no doubt he meant it. However, the hypocrisy of what church members experienced versus what we experienced could not be denied, even to my young mind. When we got home, the spigot ran dry; hugs stopped, and he fell silent.

Something had happened that I only recognized in hindsight with the wisdom of my adult years. Dad developed an idol. In a heartfelt desire to please God, he made God and ministry equal.

They are not.

Whenever we put God equal to or below something, we create an idol. Unlike God, who lovingly receives worship, idols demand it; they must be served night and day. In our case, Dad sacrificed his family on the altar of ministry. Saturdays were for sermon writing, Sundays for preaching, and Mondays, when we were in school, he took a day off.

Bible teacher and author Larry Titus recounts how he previously boasted about his hard work in ministry, rarely taking vacations, until God spoke to him: "Stop bragging; you've sinned against your family."

Dad wouldn't tolerate anything getting in the way of his idol, not even us. If a family matter could potentially compromise his image in the church, it was dealt with hastily. "Don't ruin Daddy's ministry" became a common refrain. Ministry got his best. I know many people felt love and healing through his teaching. But I also know our family suffered, and we could have been his greatest legacy of love.

Why is transparency so difficult for church leaders? I believe it's because some, *not all*, have bought into the lie of perfection. As the head, senior, or executive pastor—with prefatory titles added to the biblical preference of simply "pastor"—they falsely believe they must have it all together to minister to a church.

I don't believe it happens overnight. Most begin their journey as humble youth pastors. However, something shifts as they ascend the ranks. People find inspiration in their sermons and express their appreciation. The admiration feels good, and, as the saying goes, they start to believe their press.

Gradually, as the pressure of performing week after week sets in, so does the fear of failure. Days get longer, and tempers shorter. Where once they asked, now they demand, and nobody dares cross them. Fearing people will discover their flaws, they shrink their circle of accountability; without this, the once well-meaning pastor can fall prey to many things, including sexual temptation. Sadly, we see it on the news quite often, and the hypocrisy keeps many from attending church.

Jesus knows what lies in our hearts. Our frailty and propensity toward ego is why He declared the church His to build. We are to build the Kingdom. A Kingdom-mindset is *entirely* different: God's people are too busy representing and serving the Lord to be bothered with titles.

Our King came as a servant; He wants us to model our ways after His. Jesus said not to be like the Gentiles who lorded their authority over people. He humbled Himself, entering Jerusalem on a donkey—not on a war horse like a worldly king.

Why, then, do we need fanfare and titles? As Larry Titus says, why not be the donkey, content to carry the messenger?

———————

Hypocrisy among God's leaders is nothing new. In Biblical times, cattle were yoked together as they plowed the fields. This became an analogy for a cultural idiom: taking a rabbi's yoke meant adopting his teachings. The problem is that the rabbis demanded perfect adherence to the Law, while creating loopholes for themselves.

In contrast, Jesus told the people to take up His easy yoke; to learn from Him rather than those who imposed heavy burdens.

Even though I'd given my heart to Jesus at an early age, I struggled to connect with Him. I, too, had been unnecessarily burdened by perfection's demands. When I inevitably fell behind, I thought God was disappointed with me.

———————

As an adult, I worked at a beautiful resort. One evening, after overseeing a gala in the ballroom below, I returned to the executive offices to grab my car keys and head home. I noticed the light in my friend Sue's office and popped by to say goodnight, but stopped short when I saw Denise on her couch.

Denise and I had a choppy relationship. If I said something one way, she interpreted it another way, and vice versa. She openly shared her faith, so I knew she was a Christian. And at that point in my life, though I still loved Jesus, I didn't like His people very much. I started to back away until Sue saw me and beckoned me in.

"Denise and I are talking about my issues with Jim." I entered Sue's luxurious office, concerned. I cared about my friend and her troublesome waiting game with the man she loved.

"You alright?" I asked.

"Yes," she replied unconvincingly. Suddenly, I did something completely unpredictable. Words tumbled from my mouth before I could stop them.

"Let's pray for Sue," I said, shocking everyone, including myself. To this day, I still don't know why I said that. Perhaps the old preacher's kid instinct kicked in. More likely, out of pride, I wanted to appear pious. Either way, it was entirely unexpected.

"Um, sure!" they replied, as we formed a circle. I took their hands, as Denise added, "I'll hold your hands gently because I just got my nails done."

Can you roll your eyes to yourself? Because I know I did.

Typical, I thought, as I began offering a churchy prayer for Sue—the lengthy variety, where you say all the right things, yet there's absolutely no power. When I finished, Denise stood still, and so did Sue.

I waited. And just as I began to feel uncomfortable, Denise took her hands and placed them on either side of my head, apparently forgetting about her manicure. I felt trapped. A wave of claustrophobic panic ensued, but she persisted. To this day, we still laughingly banter about this part of the encounter. She claims to have been "lightly" touching me, while I contend that she had a vice-like grip that even a wrestler couldn't have broken; the truth is probably somewhere in between.

Then, Denise began her prayer—only two words—but undeniably powerful.

"Trust me," she said, tightening her grip. "Trust me," she repeated. Then, once more, and louder still, "Trust me." That was all.

At this moment, my world turned upside down. I envisioned a giant yoke on my shoulders, the size of a sycamore tree. Then, an even larger fist descended from heaven and shattered the yoke into a million pieces. It was irreparably damaged, but remarkably, I remained completely unharmed. Even an eternity spent trying to piece it back together would not suffice.

Before I knew it, tears poured down my cheeks. That day, God used a faithful woman to pray boldly over a broken one. I cried as my new friend, Denise, held me in her arms.

My yoke, of course, represented the countless things I believed I had to do right to please God. I hadn't realized it, but I didn't trust God. Not by a long shot. I thought He was:

- Distant and unavailable.
- Punishing me with silence.
- Uninterested in the details of my life.
- Pleased—briefly—on the rare moments I got it right.
- Irritated when I made mistakes.
- Unsympathetic to my pain.
- Unsure whether I deserved to be saved.
- Waiting to lecture me in heaven.

Who wants to serve a bully like that? Nobody, yet it was the god I served.

In my renewed pursuit of a relationship with God, I wondered how and when His image had gotten so distorted. In frustration, I grabbed a pen and a notebook to journal my thoughts. Inspired to trace the origins of my distorted beliefs, I created a chart with three columns: Dad, Mom, and God.

Next, I wrote Dad's negative and positive attributes in the column under his name. I did the same in Mom's. It took a while. Here is a sample:

Dad	Mom	God
Good Provider		
Punishes with silence		
	Unappeasable	
	Made holidays special	

Finally, God led me to put a checkmark in *His* column for each attribute I unknowingly transferred to Him. It looked like this:

Dad	Mom	God
Good Provider		✓
Punishes with silence		✓
	Unappeasable	✓
	Made holidays special	

Astounded, I realized that my parents' actions and moods shaped my perception of God. For instance, because Dad punished me with silence, I believed God did the same. However, since Dad provided for our family to the best of his ability, I felt God also provided for my needs.

Tearing down false images of God was scary. I had to replace the "mean god," as I now called him, with the *real* God. I worried that if I inadvertently chose the wrong god, I would be punished.

Not only did I receive a false image of God from my parents, but I also acquired distorted notions through religious abuse by those infiltrating a church setting. My fears manifested as panic attacks and traumatic night terrors.

I worked hard to learn the truth about God and replace the "bully" in my head. It took courage, time, and faith. And

I can assure you, just as I have not fallen from grace, neither will you.

Our God has not given us a spirit of fear, but one of love, power, and a sound mind (2 Timothy 1:7). Jesus fulfilled all the requirements of the law and left us with a new commandment: love one another as He loves us (John 13:34). He invited us into a peaceful relationship with Him and sent His Holy Spirit as a comforter to assist us.

I read my Bible with new eyes, attuned to God's love. I noted how Jesus gently lifted burdens; He didn't give them. I saw His endless compassion for people and His disciples, who were often thick-headed. I worked through my pain, layer by layer, painstakingly separating truth from lies.

I returned to church, easing myself by starting in the back row, on the end seat. I found a small community with a kind pastor. They're out there; keep looking if you don't find one immediately. Week after week, I listened to the pastor talk about grace; and week by week, I healed. God's perfect love cast out my fear.

I once saw a list about the differences between God's voice and the enemy's voice. I wish I knew who wrote it so I could credit them. It was so helpful to me on my journey, and I pray that it is for you. I have created a similar version.

God's Voice	Satan's Voice
Gentles you	Rushes you
Blesses you	Steals from you
Leads you	Pushes you
Forgives you	Condemns you
Encourages you	Shames you
Reassures you	Frightens you
Comforts you	Worries you

The next time you are tempted to believe a voice from the second column, take a long look at the first column, remembering the spirit of God's voice. Every characteristic in the first column is true of God and can be found in your Bible.

As a child, I'd sit in grassy fields and pluck the little daisies that grew. In my day, that was the "scientific" way to determine if a boy liked you in return. I'd pull petals from my flower one at a time, saying either "He loves me" or "He loves me not," hoping the last petal I tugged off ended happily: "He loves me!"

One day, I had a sweet thought. I imagined plucking a daisy God gave me; but this time, every petal said, "He loves me."

It's time to draw apart God's voice from the people who hurt you. Choose to look to Him alone; He is trustworthy, gentle, and kind. You can spend an eternity in His field of sweet-smelling flowers, and still, the last petal, the last statement, will always be...

He loves me.

CHAPTER 6

LITTLE BY LITTLE

Healing Overwhelm

I put several paint samples on the desk in front of my husband, Ted.

"Which color should we paint the living room?"

"Is this a trick question?" he replied.

"Noooo," I replied, dragging it out for effect. "Why?"

"They're all white."

"Honey!" I exclaimed. "Look closer. This one is cream, this white one has a bluish tint, and this one is bright white." He stared at the samples—and me—as I picked each one up and taped it to the wall, pointing out how the light changed the color *ever* so slightly.

"Can you see the difference now?" I asked, hopefully.

"Babe," he replied, shaking his head, "you have completely paralyzed me. I have no idea what to tell you."

We laughed. And now, when we're overwhelmed, we say, "It's all paint colors."

I am susceptible to feeling overwhelmed. Future events loom like unconquerable mountains, causing me worry. Sometimes, I worry about how much I worry. Even enjoyable things, like a trip, cause an escalating scenario of what-ifs.

- What if I don't have enough undies?
- What if the hotel doesn't have a blow-dryer?
- What if the pillow is too hard?
- What if I can hear people in the room next door?
- *What if they don't have WATER?*

Before I know it, my luggage is stuffed with inevitabilities: two bags, a gigantic cup, my pillow, and a box fan—if you know, you know. I've tried on every outfit, packed for a heat wave *and* a snowstorm, and ensured my comfy socks are tucked into my purse. All that's left is to check that I turned off the stove... and find a U-Haul for all my things.

Perhaps it's a byproduct of anxiety stemming from childhood trauma. Unbeknownst to me, on a cognitive level, I developed the belief that if something could go wrong, it would.

When I worry about the outcome of a decision, I feel compelled to run a mental playlist of every negative outcome before getting started, as if to prepare myself. It's exhausting. I often talk myself out of an adventure or, even worse, a dream. Those kinds of what-ifs stifle inspiration.

- What if people discover I don't know what I'm doing?
- What if they don't like what I've done?
- What if people are mean?
- What if nobody identifies with my work?

In those cases, fear usually wins out. It locks the door to my dreams and paralyzes me.

It took many attempts to begin my writing journey. Stopping and starting repeatedly on my own, I finally found a group of women and joined their writer's critique group.

The first time I presented my work, my hands shook—I

had to sit on them to control the trembling. I spent at least five minutes urging them to be truthful before allowing them to start. They smiled patiently and read the introduction of the book that you now hold in your hands. Rather than shunning my work, they embraced it. One friend's eyes filled with tears as she recalled the pain of her childhood. At that moment, I realized something profound.

Although I always prepared myself for negative outcomes, I *never* prepared myself for a positive one.

And so, I encourage you to dream again, to imagine new possibilities:

- What if the project you're working on changes lives, even if—or especially if—it's your own life that changes?
- What if everything goes smoothly?
- What if you enjoy it and make new friends?
- *What if it's good?*

Breaking free can be challenging; but a generation in the Bible managed to do it. Their examples and lessons are still relevant today.

After God delivered the Israelites from slavery, they wandered in the Sinai Desert for forty years. There they remained, torn between returning to their captors and moving forward into the perils of an unknown land—stuck between the past and the future. The entire generation passed away bereft, even after witnessing miracles like the parting of the Red Sea, water flowing from rocks, and daily bread given in the form of manna from heaven.

While they gained physical freedom from their captors, they never achieved the emotional or spiritual freedom necessary to enter the abundance of the Promised Land. It's heart-breaking to think about.

Under Joshua's leadership, the next generation prepared to take the land. The sheer enormity of the battle could have paralyzed them, yet God provided Joshua with a strategy.

God said, "You shall not be terrified of [your enemies]; for the Lord your God, the great and awesome God, is among you. And the Lord your God will drive out those nations before you little by little; you will be unable to destroy them at once, lest the beasts of the field become too numerous for you." (Deuteronomy 7:21-22).

This God-given direction included two of the greatest keys to overcoming fear of the unknown and healing overwhelm.

First, God warned them not to dread their enemies. We are highly susceptible to dread when we look into the future.

There's a beautiful aquarium in Monterey, a city on California's rugged coastline. The aquarium is committed to education and preservation. Massive habitats were created to house the living sea creatures. My favorite exhibit is a two-story tank filled with waving green strands of kelp, fish of every variety, and reef sharks.

One day, as I put a concerning matter to prayer, I saw myself—from a distance—*in* the tank *with* the sharks. Then, as if pressing a zoom button, I saw the image again, but up close. I noticed I wasn't in the tank but was standing in front of it, simply admiring. That is quite a difference of danger versus beauty.

When we focus on the future, we are prone to project dread and fear. We picture ourselves in the shark tank. Yet, our future experience is often completely different, filled with joys undreamed of.

Have you ever noticed that our enemies—fear and doubt—mostly lurk in the future?

That's because they can't kill dreams in this moment.

God uses our steps of faith today, in this moment, to clear the way for us tomorrow.

———————————

The second strategy is one of my favorites. God promised to clear away the nations little by little, to contain the wild beasts that roamed the land. The people were outnumbered by the beasts; the Israelites could not yet care for all He would give them. Rather than taking all the land immediately, they were to move forward, multiply, and move forward again.

In the meantime, God used the enemy nations to control the wild beasts on their behalf. What an incredible concept! Isn't it exciting to think somebody might be taking care of something meant for you?

You don't need to have anxiety or fear. God will protect what awaits you.

If God knows we must take things gradually, why do we attempt to conquer everything at once? It is a recipe for disaster. We are only responsible for the first step. Once we grow, we can take another step.

Radio host and author Dave Ramsey has a formula for this: "Focused intensity over time multiplied by God's blessing equals unstoppable momentum."[1]

When I discovered this principle, I began to focus on manageable steps I could take. I asked God to show me where to start, so I could move forward into His promises for me. Unsurprisingly, He started me with small steps.

———————————

1   https://x.com/DaveRamsey/status/773110841730338816 3:49AM, Sep 6, 2016

Writing a book felt unattainable. But God had me begin with a daily journal entry. At first, I had little to say, scribbling only a line or two, sometimes as simple as "Good morning, Jesus." I won't lie, it felt futile; but many years later, I was writing pages at a time. I had become practiced at writing without realizing it. And even more surprising, I loved it.

Since I carried my diary everywhere, I was grateful not to miss the moment when God began to speak to me unexpectedly. On the morning of our last vacation day in Hawaii, Teddy and I sat on the beach, watching the waves gently lap the shore. The sand felt cool beneath my feet, and a warm breeze carrying the scent of plumerias caressed my face. So peaceful. I dug out my notebook from my beach bag and spread it on my lap. With a pen in one hand and coffee in the other, I decided to dream a bit. After jotting down a list of desires, I paused. That's when God shared His desire for me to do more with my writing. I asked Him to provide the opportunity.

Within months, Larry Titus asked me to partner with him on a book idea. We produced the book—as well as another!—over the next eighteen months.

Do you have a big goal? Pray for the first step. Break your promise into a daily discipline. There's no age limit. Jesus waited thirty years to begin His public ministry. At the time of this writing, I am in my sixtieth year.

Dreams don't have an expiration date when we keep them alive by faith.

And what does it matter if somebody is doing something similar? God is not asking for worldly uniqueness, He is asking for you to share His love. What you produce will be an entirely unique expression of your faith. The world needs what you have to offer.

————————

I've heard people attribute their financial success to making their bed every morning. While I certainly wouldn't be upset with that outcome, I make my bed daily for a more personal reason.

Most days, before my feet hit the floor, I already battle emotional overwhelm. Making my bed helps calm those anxious feelings. I stretch the sheets tightly over the corners, smooth the cover, and fluff the duvet. Somehow, I feel better. A small step, which takes just minutes, benefits my mental health throughout the day, as it inevitably leads to my next task.

In Acts, chapter 9, the apostle Peter visited the city of Lydda, where he met a paralyzed man. As the story goes, Peter says, "Aeneas, Jesus Christ heals you; rise and make your bed" (Acts 9:34, ESV). Aeneas immediately rose; his chronic and crippling ailment miraculously healed. Why is this the first thing Peter had him do? Shouldn't he let the man run around and celebrate first? I know I'd want to.

Scholars have many theories about this. For instance, when Jesus healed the paralyzed man, he told him to pick up his mat and walk. The mat represented his former lifestyle as a beggar, which he could now leave behind. They say Peter followed Jesus's example. Others suggest Peter wanted the man to put his healing into effective action.

While I don't discount these, I have a thought of my own. Just as bad things can feel overwhelming, good things can, too. Sometimes, I've been *positively* overwhelmed by the kindness of loving friends at celebrations.

Perhaps, as wonderful as it felt to be healed, the simple act of rolling up his mat, of doing something small and modest that he had been unable to do, stabilized the overwhelming sensations within the man.

The miraculous paved the way for the ordinary, because the ordinary is, in itself, miraculous.

———————

The Bible has other examples of people performing simple chores immediately after they're healed. Jesus resurrected a little girl and then asked her parents to bring her something to eat. When He healed Peter's mother-in-law, the first thing she did was prepare a meal.

There's just something about performing basic activities that can ground us after emotional events. My friend immediately cleans the house when her grown children leave for college. It helps her cope with feelings of loneliness.

Sometimes, feelings of overwhelm make it difficult to know where to begin. When my daughter was little, her room sometimes got very messy, looking like a toy tornado had swept through. I didn't just say, "Clean your room." I knew from experience that wouldn't be effective.

Instead, I told her *how* to start: "Let's make the bed; that always makes things look better." We then sorted the toys into similar piles: stuffed animals in one pile, dolls in another, and so on. The task became simple, and I left her alone to finish returning the toys to their appropriate bins.

Our minds are no different. When the day feels overwhelming, we can make it simpler by creating a to-do list and, if it helps, organizing it by category. Start by completing just one task, and see how you feel. Be kind to yourself. Zechariah 4:10 says not to despise small beginnings.

Small things grow.

Jesus said God's kingdom is like a tiny mustard seed that becomes a large tree, or like a microscopic grain of yeast in dough that has the power to make the whole loaf rise. He told parables about little things like coins and pearls. He chose twelve disciples, not one hundred. He multiplied one boy's lunch to feed thousands. He spoke of the goodness of giving a stranger a cup of water—just one cup.

———————

Small, kind acts have the power to change the world. And in one's personal life, these acts can repel negativity and diffuse anxiety.

They embody acts of grace.

One day, I sat in the drive-through line at a coffee shop, waiting my turn to move forward. I got caught up in reading a text, leading to a slight gap forming between my car and the car in front of me. Not a major concern, I thought, since there were still two cars ahead of me. The man behind me didn't agree. He honked his truck horn loudly and continuously. I nearly jumped out of my skin, my cell phone flying to the floor. I picked it up and drove the short distance to the next car. When I finally reached the window, my hands were shaking. The barista leaned out the window and asked kindly, "Wow, are you okay?"

"I'm not sure, but I think we need to teach him a lesson." I could tell she liked the idea from the grin on her face.

"What should we do?" she asked gleefully.

"I'm going to buy his coffee," I replied, "and teach him a lesson in grace."

She looked at me quizzically; then, the lightbulb went on. "Great idea." I paid the bill, which was minimal, waved goodbye to my co-conspirator, and drove away.

I've often wondered about that man. I like to believe my lesson became part of a seed of change in him. In the book of Zechariah, God instructs us to speak grace to the mountain, which will be reduced to nothing. When we are kind and extend grace, we release God's power into our circumstances. Perhaps the man's anger melted away in the face of kindness; I'll never know. But I know his anger did not take hold of me, and that's empowering enough.

After making my bed in the morning, I prepare my coffee. I carefully measure the delicious -smelling grounds from the sparkling glass canisters I found at a flea market. While the coffee brews, I select a seasonally inspired mug from our collection and add some monk fruit, relishing the grainy sound. My first sip always brings a smile to my face. So simple; so delightful.

Jesus came to give us abundant life. He takes pleasure in simple joys and ordinary tasks. During His time on Earth, He dined in friends' homes, prepared breakfast by a comforting fire for His disciples, and walked along country roads, teaching them His ways.

On the contrary, evil, by its nature, aims to overwhelm. The enemy seeks to drown out life within God's beautiful children. He convinces us that we are worthless unless we accomplish something sensational. Or, using another tactic, he instills so much fear that we never begin.

The next time you're overwhelmed—and buying into the lie that nothing you do matters and your day is destined to fail—take a small step. Remember the power of little things and God's delight in ordinary acts.

Embrace the small steps. It doesn't matter where or how you begin; just beginning is enough.

CHAPTER 7

HIDDEN IN HIM

Healing Grief

I grew up in South Africa during the Apartheid, a diabolical and turbulent time in the country's history. We had a lovely park opposite our home, where my friends and I enjoyed playing. The leafy green trees, fragrant flowers, swings, and seesaws set a beautiful stage for families. However, at times, it became a scene of violence. Riots broke out, with people yelling fiercely until police sirens dispersed the mobs. But even after the park resumed its quiet appearance, who would want to play there anymore?

Nobody, that's who.

———————

I sat opposite a woman and listened as she shared the pain of her marriage. Her husband was prone to yelling. When challenged, he escalated further; if she tried to walk away, he goaded her. Later, repentant, he would apologize and promise not to do it again. When she naturally pulled away after his episodes, he accused her of being unforgiving—a no-win situation.

The woman falsely believed that since his rage was verbal, rather than physical, she didn't have the right to leave, erect boundaries or seek help to keep herself safe. She felt herself shutting down and wondered if her response was typical. My park came to mind.

I said, "Picture a beautiful meadow filled with scented flowers and a trickling stream. Would you enjoy strolling through it?"

"Yes," she replied.

"What if I told you that a riot would erupt at any moment? It's not a matter of if, but when. Do you still want to walk there?"

"No."

"Why not?"

"Because I don't want to get hurt."

"In the same way," I assured her, "your husband's rage is unsafe. You don't know what will trigger it or when, so you are constantly on guard, even when things seem peaceful. Of course you do not want to re-engage. Living in fear of rage is not living; it is not the abundant life Jesus died to give us, and you do not have to continue enduring this." Thankfully, she received professional care.

Another friend's volatile father had an oppressive impact on the entire family. When the dad came home from work in a happy mood, they all breathed a sigh of relief. If he came home angry, the family walked on eggshells to avoid further enraging him. An influential person set the temperature in their home. Even when things felt peaceful again, my friend feared things would escalate. As an adult, loud noises still frighten and trigger him.

It's worth restating—who wants to live like that?

Nobody, that's who.

Volatile environments breed fear and, ultimately, unhealthy coping mechanisms. I still remember the panic that would course through my body like a bolt of hot lightning whenever I saw my father's jaw clench or watched him leap from his chair.

With a heightened fight-or-flight response, I became conflict-avoidant, hiding like an ostrich and waiting for the storm to pass. At other times, I became conflict-aggressive. I later called these two tendencies stuffing and raging.

When we feel unsafe expressing our feelings, we may stuff and suppress them. However, they will inevitably manifest through unhealthy releases. Numbing our pain can lead to overdrinking, overdosing, overeating, overspending, over-controlling behaviors, and overreacting.

Think of it like a field of Jello. If you stomp down on one area, you may squish it flat, but it will push upward somewhere else. Pain will manifest. The only solution is to heal the root cause.

A year into our marriage, my husband and I invited our mentors, Larry and Devi Titus, to have dinner at our home. Ted and I were experiencing a challenging season. Both of us had emerged from broken pasts, and as we wove our story together, some pieces didn't align easily. We knew God had brought us together, so why was it so difficult?

Larry and Devi invited transparency. Over dinner, we shared our stories. I didn't hide my pain, nor did Teddy conceal his confusion about why he behaved as he did. Larry gave one correction to Ted. One.

Devi then gave me an exhortation that rivaled that of the prophet Amos. She told me that regardless of how I *felt*, I did not get to speak disrespectfully to Teddy. While I thought change began with others, it actually started with me, Devi insisted. She spoke kindly but firmly. I wasn't accustomed to being confronted in such a direct manner; she had my attention.

Thus began my journey of ownership: to address and heal my porous character traits. That night, through tears, I recognized the truth—I needed to grow up and stop justifying my actions. Adults should not respond with reactionary behavior.

I became disrespectful when I felt hurt by my husband; it was how I coped as a child, my only weapon then. While disdain may have been better than the violence I grew up with, it was neither loving nor Christlike. By setting aside my core value of kindness whenever I lost respect for someone, I became undignified and caused them reproach.

The morning after our encounter, I called Devi. She answered immediately and was incredibly loving. Until her exhortation, I hadn't realized I could live a powerful life despite all that had happened to me. I will never forget her reassuring words. She quoted Psalm 30:5: "Weeping may endure for a night, but joy comes in the morning."

In time, Ted received healing for his depression through a doctor's care, and I received therapy for my emotional wounds. Our marriage thrived. Not long ago, as I sat at my desk, I felt him staring at me from the corner of my eye.

"Yes?" I asked, looking up from my task.

His eyes were filled with tears. "Thank you," he said.

"For what, honey?"

"When Devi corrected you, it wasn't all you. I didn't know that at the time. But when you changed, it forced me to confront my behavior. You've never turned back. I'm so grateful."

The change he referred to was when I started owning

my behavior. I worked on eliminating that which no longer served who I wanted to be. In the process, I learned some powerful truths about anger:

- It is okay to feel anger.
- It is okay to express my feelings firmly and respectfully.
- It is okay to take time out when I no longer feel in control of myself.

I chose kindness during conflict. I began confronting situations in ways that benefited others while honoring my principles. My past no longer dictated my present. I grew.

We are responsible for treating those we love kindly.

When we calm our emotions and stop the reactionary outbursts, our souls quiet long enough to recognize what lies beneath the anger—a tender and painful grief.

When I faced my grief for the first time, I began to understand why it sought my attention through anger. I could hardly believe that my raw, fragile, and vulnerable grief had survived unseen for so long. It was like finding a lonely child hidden in the corner. I sat with that child for a long time, listening to her stories of abandonment and weeping over her—over our—lost childhood. I cried for months.

I asked Jesus, "Where were you? Why did you let those things happen? Why didn't you rescue me?" Ever so gently, He reminded me of my olive jar incident.

While opening an olive jar, the glass beneath the lid unexpectedly shattered, lacerating my fingertip. I won't go into details, but it hurt. Even after it healed, the resulting scar tissue bothered me. I thought about it every day. Such a small part, yet my whole body was aware of it.

Jesus then reminded me about the Apostle Paul. Before his conversion, he sought to annihilate Christians. With permission from the authorities to jail or kill Christ's followers, he pursued them to Damascus. As he approached the city, a blinding light from heaven stopped him. Jesus stood between him and his victims, saying, "Saul, Saul, why do you persecute me?" (Acts 9:4).

Paul later wrote that we are the body of Christ. I believe his awareness was rooted in this encounter. Jesus knows everything that happens to His body. When Paul persecuted God's children, he persecuted Jesus. Even if you feel insignificant, like "just a fingertip," so to speak, you are not insignificant to Him.

When we feel something, He feels it, too. What happens to us happens to Jesus.

During our brief time on this Earth, God is invisible to us. But we never step outside of His body. Because of His Son's sacrifice, we are tucked inside His heart; we have *become* His body, and He is fully aware of everything that happens to us. After all, He named His Son Immanuel—God with us.

I understood this better when I became a mother. The nurses handed me my little bundle, and I instantly tucked my daughter inside my arms. I didn't sleep a wink in the hospital, I was on staring duty.

I stroked her cheek through the night, held her hand in the baby warmer, kissed her fuzzy head, and repeatedly told her, "I love you, I love you, I love you." As she grew, my heart broke with every boo-boo, whether a tumble or a heartbreak.

I once heard, "Having a child is like watching your heart walk around outside your body." How true this is.

I wish I knew why Jesus waited until people were thrown in prison and murdered before intervening against Paul. I wish I knew why He waited so long to rescue me. Or you. And while I may not have the answer to those painful questions, I do have this answer: Jesus felt it, He saw it, and He will restore every wrong done to you, His beloved child.

For you are not His heart walking around outside His body; you are tucked within it, eternally.

PART THREE

GROWING FROM YOUR STORY

CHAPTER 8

TEAM LATRINE

Healing Bitterness

As mentioned, I worked at a beautiful resort with demanding clientele. Meeting their high expectations required a lot of work. Sometimes, at the end of a long day, I leaned against my friend's office door to complain.

One evening, after listening to another of my rants, he calmly asked, "Bitter, table for one?" This made us both laugh and became our running joke.

The truth is, nobody wants to be around bitter people. Sooner or later, they eat alone.

I'll never forget the day my nephew, only a toddler at the time, encountered his first lemon. He watched intently as my sister placed the enticing yellow slices on a plate. Before we could stop him, he grabbed one and stuffed it into his mouth. His whole body shuddered, and he pursed his lips. He quickly pulled out the offending fruit with his chubby fist and stared at it confusedly.

To our surprise, he licked it again, as if double-checking—*still* bitter. After the same result in round two, his experiment was over for good.

Bitter people and situations are like that. When encountering them, we recoil in surprise or attempt to metabolize the strange occurrence.

After church one Sunday, Ted saw a friend in the long line of cars exiting the parking lot and ran to greet him. The friend was pleased, but not the couple behind him. The man laid on the horn to express his frustration with the brief inconvenience. I couldn't believe my eyes—we had just left church, for heaven's sake! Their faces were so sour; I can still picture them today.

These "living lemons" find fault with everyone, though seemingly oblivious to their own shortcomings. At their mildest, they're sour and annoying. At their worst, they can crush dreams.

———————

There's a woman in the Bible called Naomi. Her name means pleasant and gentle. She moved with her husband, Elimelech, and their two sons from Jerusalem to Moab to seek relief during a famine.

While there, her sons married the Gentiles Ruth and Orpah. In a tragic turn of events, her husband and sons died, leaving the three women bereft. Upon learning that the famine had ended, Naomi decided to return home. The Bible tells us that when the women in her hometown, Bethlehem, greeted her, she replied, "Do not call me Naomi; call me Mara, for the Almighty has dealt very bitterly with me" (Ruth 1:20).

Her reference to Marah, an oasis in the wilderness, would not have been lost on her friends. After escaping their bondage in Egypt, the Israelites tried to drink the water from the oasis but found it bitter, hence the name.

Here is the thing about bitterness. The Israelites did not know from looking at the water that it was bitter. They had to taste it first. At some point, we will all taste bitterness; it doesn't mean we have done something wrong.

The key is not to swallow it.

If we do, the Bible tells us, it will become a root embedded in our souls, bearing sour fruit.

To make the oasis water sweet, Moses threw some wood into it. Through his act of faith, God changed the properties of the water and healed them. Faith is the key to transformation. We must carefully define things through the long-term perspective of faith rather than our momentary feelings.

———————

I don't know when the acidic seeds first embedded in Naomi—Mara—but her story offers a clue. Years earlier, she named her sons Mahlon and Chilion, meaning "sickly" and "wasting." Perhaps she had a difficult time during childbirth and attributed this pain to her children. We can only guess. But when the Bible relates their death, are we surprised? They lived out the destiny of their ominous names.

Nobody can blame Naomi for grieving the loss of her children. However, she allowed bitterness to redefine her, even to the point of changing her name.

In problematic seasons, I've heard people express that they hate their life, a life Jesus died to save. I wish they understood how damaging such statements are to their soul and those of us who love them. Perhaps if they did, they might choose their words differently.

At eighteen weeks pregnant, after a routine ultrasound to

discern the gender of our baby, the doctor informed me I had a condition that indicated possible congenital disabilities and counseled me to consider options.

That day, Ted and I named our child Zoe—a Greek name that means "life." Five months later, our daughter was born without complications, but we had already decided to bless her with a life-giving name, whatever the outcome. Names are so important. We must designate our loved ones and seasons well.

Proverbs 18:21 tells us that the power of life and death resides in our tongue. This is not a "name it and claim it" philosophy. It's wisdom.

As Naomi prepared to return home, her daughters-in-law Ruth and Orpah begged to accompany her but were refused repeatedly:

> Turn back, my daughters; why will you go with me? Have I yet sons in my womb that they may become your husbands? Turn back, my daughters; go your way, for I am too old to have a husband. If I should say I have hope, even if I should have a husband this night and should bear sons, would you therefore wait till they were grown... No, my daughters, for it is exceedingly bitter to me for your sake that the hand of the Lord has gone out against me (Ruth 1:11-13).

Although Ruth and Orpah also experienced loss, Naomi does not offer them comfort. Her words are filled with hopelessness and, dare I say, sarcasm.

I understand Naomi's sorrow. I truly do. However, this dear woman faced a long-standing issue. Just as she had given her sons faithless names, she spoke faithlessly about the future. Naomi succumbed to self-pity. Where God had placed a comma in her story, she put a period.

Naomi's speech about her plight provides a valuable starting point for our own reflection, whether we have allowed the root of bitterness to take hold in our hearts. Consider these questions:

- What do I name situations and people in my life?
- Do I believe I am destined for a life of hopelessness?
- Do I doubt my circumstances will ever change?
- Do I push others away?
- Do I complain, using sarcastic words?
- Do I believe God has turned His back on me?
- Am I genuinely seeking answers or just ranting?
- Do I blame others for my lot in life?

We may easily identify a friend or relative who embodies these traits. But do we see them in ourselves? It's an important question to consider.

Naomi's daughter-in-law, Orpah, whose name means "fawn," begged to go on. Perhaps she'd heard Naomi speak about Jerusalem and the God she worshipped, and longed to see her homeland. Perhaps she simply yearned for a fresh start. But at some point, Fawn, in her scared innocence, turned back. She kissed her mother-in-law goodbye and left.

Have you ever been eager to experience new things? Perhaps you shared your hopes with someone, only to be met with negativity. Did their caustic response turn you from your path, burying your dream? Bitterness crushed Orpah's desire, and she is never heard of again.

However, Naomi did not count on Ruth.

I've heard Ruth's response to Naomi recited calmly at weddings. Although I can't prove it, I believe Ruth stood her ground and passionately expressed the following words. It plays out in my mind much like a scene from The Chosen. I can almost see the tears streaming down her cheeks as she emboldenedly speaks:

> *Do not urge me to leave you or to return from following you. For where you go I will go, and where you lodge I will lodge. Your people shall be my people, and your God my God. Where you die I will die, and there will I be buried. May the Lord do so to me and more also if anything but death parts me from you (Ruth 1:16-17).*

Her response silenced Naomi. Why? Well, first, Ruth established a boundary by telling her *what not to do*: "Do not urge me to leave..."

Second, she stated what she, Ruth, *would do*, declaring her plans in a prudent series of "I will" statements.

Third, she made herself answerable to God, taking the matter out of Naomi's hands.

Ruth had nothing left to live for in Moab. She'd buried her husband and chosen her mother-in-law's God. Her new life awaited in Jerusalem, and that was that. By faith, she saw a future and moved toward it.

Has God given you a promise? Hold on to it dearly. Only He knows the future. Ruth's faith held a great reward, which we will discover in the next chapter. She empowered herself to rise above her pain-filled past, believing in God for more.

I chatted with a woman after her encounter with a bitter person; she looked like she had survived a hit-and-run incident. Her dreams shattered, she couldn't comprehend why all hope appeared lost. She resembled a helpless fawn, ready to flee. I told her this story.

I worked at a kids' camp during college, and my co-counselor didn't like me. I couldn't change that, so she was stuck with me for the summer. The camp culminated in a three-day canoe excursion. During a general assembly attended by everyone, the counselors were assigned their chores for the trip.

My co-counselor discovered that my friend and I would be assigned the worst job of all: digging toilets. She leaned back in delight to watch our reaction. However, before the announcement, she made the mistake of letting it slip to a camper, who ran to tell me. Thanks to the tip-off, we had time to prepare.

In a stroke of genius, we decided to spin the narrative. When they announced toilet duty, the kids looked at us concerned, but we leaped from our seats, shouting, "Yes! Team Latrine! Who's with us?" Campers clamored to join. High fives all around.

Call me ornery, but we didn't stop there.

We created the flag of destiny—a spade with a long strand of toilet paper tied to the handle that flapped in the wind. At each stop, we led a brigade to the top of a hill, bearing our flag and singing annoyingly as we dug the loo. Reports came back that my co-counselor was fuming. Shame on me for enjoying the shenanigans I caused; but as silly as it may be, the story teaches a valuable lesson.

For reasons known only to her, my co-counselor swallowed the bitterness bug. It tainted her summer, but not mine. I should have thanked her for teaching me a valuable lesson. I'd probably have groaned in despair if I hadn't been tipped off. Instead, my positive reaction inspired many campers, even if I only did it so she wouldn't get the best of me.

Here's the truth: Bitterness is an enemy, but that doesn't mean it has to define you. You still have the power to cultivate a positive perspective and rewrite your story. You can keep your dream alive, even if it is simply to enjoy the last days of summer with a bunch of goofy, adorable kids.

Ruth connected herself to God and, against all odds, transformed her life. She reclaimed her power, not by exerting it over others but by empowering herself with faith. Life gave her lemons, but she added sweetness and made lemonade.

Some individuals take pleasure in seeing others brought low. They are moved by a worldly spirit. What if you choose a different response than they expect? Not out of spite but for a godly purpose. Try a new tactic: grab a spade, make a flag, climb your hill, and spread joy. Joy is contagious.

When my friend heard my camp story, she smiled through tears. Although she'd been hurt in encountering negativity from someone she loved, she felt empowered knowing she had the authority to dictate her response. As is common, the person who hurt her had experienced a loss and was not her best self. In the context of empowering ourselves, we must be prepared to give people grace.

We discussed ways for her to implement Ruth's formula: lovingly create boundaries, decide what *she* wanted, and leave the rest to God. The next day, I received a text: "I walked out of our time together a little taller." I like that. Walk taller. As I see it, we have three choices in the face of bitterness:

1. Like Naomi, we can swallow it and bear its fruit.
2. Like Orpah, we can cut short our desires and leave no known legacy.
3. Like Ruth, we can lovingly stand our ground and move forward into God's promise.

I know what I choose. I'll go with Ruth's choice—mixed with a sassy touch of Team Latrine.

CHAPTER 9

LET YOUR EYES BE ON THIS FIELD

Healing Comparison

When searching for an affordable family home, a new build was not an option, given our budget and the high prices of California real estate. This meant we had to find a fixer-upper and buy at a low enough price to save money for initial renovations. It took some time, but eventually, we found our house; and sure enough, it needed a lot of work.

For reasons unknown, the front door was painted a peculiar shade of pink and bubbled with blisters. Inside, the situation wasn't much better. A strange mural depicting two hands linked together decorated the guest bathroom—a conversation starter for sure—and random shades of green and brown paint adorned the walls. The kitchen counter resembled a saloon pull-up bar. A courtyard overgrown with weeds and bushes stood at the center of the home, where mosquitoes buzzed merrily in a favorable habitat. And the backyard was a strange blend of swamp and desert.

"We'll take it!" I said to our agent and longtime friend.

"I knew you would," he smiled.

We took our young daughter to see the house, and her face fell. She was devastated to hear that the mosquito breeding ground—the only thing she liked, because it felt like a forest—would be cleared.

"My darling," I said, "trust Mommy. You'll see."

Ultimately, we got such a good deal that I had enough money to tear up the stained carpet, put in new floors, and remove the saloon counter. We painted everything creamy white. Landscapers cleared the courtyard and laid cost-efficient gray pea gravel until we could afford to do more. My friends thought it looked like a charming French patio.

Before we knew it, move-in day arrived. Because the construction team was still working on the kitchen, I set up a buffet in the dining area, similar to a bed and breakfast, for Zoe to choose her cereal in the morning. She loved it.

Years later, she wrote a school essay about the adventure. She described her amazement with the transformation. When she saw our renewed home, fresh from its facelift, it became her new favorite place.

As a child, she couldn't yet see the potential I saw. Beneath the paint and repairs lay a diamond in the rough.

In the chapter on bitterness, we encounter Ruth at a crossroads. Leaving behind her former life and everything familiar, she steps into an uncertain future alongside her mother-in-law, Naomi, to begin anew. The two women arrive in Bethlehem during the barley harvest of spring.

With Naomi's blessing, Ruth began gleaning in the fields for grain. Jewish law required farmers to leave the corners of the field unharvested, providing sustenance for the poor. By chance, she gleaned in the field of Naomi's relative, Boaz.

Watching Ruth from a distance, Boaz inquired about her from his men. Hearing about her situation and her hard work in the field, Boaz was inspired to approach Ruth. After advising her to stay close to the other women, he said, "Let your eyes be on the field which they reap, and go after them" (Ruth 2:9).

Like the story of our home, the grain field probably didn't appear very promising initially. Picture endless rows of tightly planted barley stretching beneath the hot sun. Like wheat, barley has sharp stems that can cause paper-like cuts, not to mention the back-breaking work of bending over to pick up bundles of sheaves. Plus, I imagine she saw a rodent or two scampering underneath—eek!

But divine providence had placed Ruth there, and Boaz wasn't done blessing her. He promised protection from his workers and water from their vessels. His fields became a safe haven.

———

I had the most wonderful and sweet aunt. When I visited her home, my safe place, she would create a magical world for me, telling stories of fairies while feeding me mounds of toast with jam. I often wondered how she could be filled so with love and joy.

Years later, she stayed at my home, and I had the blessing of serving her. When I made her a cup of tea, just regular tea, she thanked me as if I'd deposited a million dollars into her bank account. When I wrapped her with a blanket, she touched my hand and said, "Thank you so much, my darling." In those moments, I discovered the secret to her joy: gratitude. Her grateful heart made me want to give her the world.

When Ruth heard Boaz's promise to protect her and provide her with water—two very simple favors—she fell at his feet. Like my aunt, Ruth also possessed a grateful heart. The smallest gestures inspired great thankfulness.

I am sure this moved Boaz's heart even more. Did he also want to give her the world? Perhaps, because soon after, he invited her to lunch and ordered the workers to leave even more barley for her to glean.

That evening, Ruth returned home to Naomi, who wisely recognized favor when she saw it. Naomi held her tongue and waited until the kind man finished barley season before she began their matchmaking.

It appears our dear Naomi emerged from her bitter season. We see in her a newfound care for her daughter-in-law's well-being. No longer self-focused, she suggested Ruth make her intentions known to Boaz by lying at his feet while he slept. When Boaz awoke, he commended her act and sent her on her way. On that same day, he made plans to marry her.

Eventually, they had a son named Obed, who became the grandfather of King David in the lineage of Jesus. It turns out there was more than just barley in Ruth's field. It contained:

- Protection
- Provision
- Inheritance
- Her husband
- A beloved son
- A role in Christ's redemptive story

Talk about a diamond in the rough. I'm so grateful Ruth did not compare her field to another more promising one. Imagine what she would have missed out on.

You've probably heard the phrase, "Comparison is the thief of joy." As tempting as it is to let our eyes linger on someone else's life or their possessions—we must realize the grass is not always greener. We don't know what struggles others face behind closed doors. Comparative insecurity harms us and our relationships.

Author and speaker Shawna Marie Bryant tells a story about this in her book *Longing to Belong*. After posing for a promo picture with several speakers, including me, for an upcoming event, she stepped away from the group. I caught up to her and asked if she was okay.

"Not really," she replied, "I just look at all these beautiful women, and I feel ugly, fat, and old."

"Oh," I mused, "a UFO sighting."

"A UFO?" she asked, her brow puckering.

"Yes, *ugly, fat, old*." Despite feeling rotten, she laughed. I then assured her there was no truth to UFOs—that I know of—and neither was there any truth to the lie she believed. I went on to name her many wonderful attributes.

Even more upsetting, what if she hadn't told me her struggle? It could have interfered with her relationships and kept her from community, possibly even from public speaking. I wonder how many treasures have been lost by internalized insecurity. I'm so glad my friend humbly shared her heart.

Growing up, we didn't have much, but we had a roof over our heads and three meals a day. My clothes were donated, or we made them. Although Dad worked hard, we couldn't afford college for me. But, through an unimaginable gift, a generous benefactor gave me a scholarship to attend a Texas school.

I felt like the most blessed human alive. I thought my cup couldn't overflow any more, until I met Texans—they were all so kind and friendly! And, as it turned out, wealthy.

I took rides in my friends' brand-new cars to spend the day at their parents' mansions. They tossed beautiful clothes onto dorm room floors—garments that would have taken me months to afford—and designer bags draped their arms. Meanwhile, I didn't even know there was such a thing as a designer bag. In just a few short months, my overflowing cup suddenly felt empty. My kind friends never made me feel less than; the struggle was all my own. I looked at their lovely clothes, then at my threadbare garments. I wasn't jealous; instead, I felt ashamed.

In the game of comparison, we either win or lose. There is no middle ground.

When we compare ourselves to others, we will feel one of two things: shame for what we lack or pride for what we possess. If we're being honest, we have probably felt both—it's an emotional rollercoaster.

There are days I've taken time to do my hair and makeup and hopped in the car feeling pretty cute. Then, upon arriving to my location, I've spotted a stunning natural beauty who rolled out of bed looking amazing—"pretty cute" flies out the window pretty quick.

Friends, we are in bad shape if our emotional barometer is based on temperamental traits like appearances. God does not desire His children to yearn for things or relationships not meant for us, and He certainly never wants us to feel shame.

———————

Do you remember the first thing Adam and Eve did in the garden after they sinned in Genesis 3? Driven by shame, they made garments from fig leaves and hid. These inadequate coverings would never do, so God killed an animal and covered them with its skin. It was the first sign of the blood covering to come.

What if they—what if I—had chosen to talk to God instead of hiding in shame? Like Eve, and unlike Ruth, I began to focus on what I *didn't* have rather than what I did. Driven by a fear of scarcity, rooted in comparison, I pursued materialism and wandered into fields that God never intended for me. I got lost for a while.

When I finally recognized my folly, I begged God to forgive and restore me. I prayed a bold prayer: "Dear God, I only want what you have for me, even if nothing remains, regardless of the cost."

In His mercy, the God of second chances answered. He removed it all. Nothing remained of the life I'd built for myself since college. Although there was sorrow, I didn't mind; I was finally free. I used what money I had to attend a seminary in Southern California full time.

With new priorities, I spent mornings on my surfboard and afternoons in class. Then, after three years, I felt God say, *Your husband is watching you. You might want to dress a little nicer.* I laughed out loud. Looking down at my grungy sweats, I couldn't agree more.

Unbeknownst to me, Ted had fallen in love with me during our class on the Gospel of John.

While I focused on my work, he focused on me.

With the *thief of joy* rooted out of my life, my happiness caught his attention. On the day I began dressing up, he watched me from a classroom window and decided he'd waited long enough to ask me out. The rest, as they say, is history.

———————

After Ruth thanked Boaz for his kindness, she couldn't help but ask why. He responded that he knew she'd left her country, been kind to her mother-in-law, and had the confidence to move to a place she knew nothing about.

In other words, while she focused on her work, he kept his eyes on her.

I understand the distraction of the things of this world. I've fought that battle, and probably will again. I'm looking at you, Instagram. But I have never regretted the times I've peeled my gaze away and focused on the things that matter to Jesus. Even if it looks like a deserted, sun-scorched barley field, God will surely have surprises hidden there on our behalf.

When we drop comparison and run after the things of God, in the words of Boaz, "The LORD [will] repay your work, and a full reward be given you by the LORD God of Israel, under whose wings you have come for refuge" (Ruth 2:12).

God watches us, not to find fault but to reward us. Even if somebody else's field looks better than ours, we can trust where He has placed us. Find refuge beneath His wings; it is where you will hear His loving heartbeat.

And *nothing* compares to that.

CHAPTER 10

OPEN GATES, WOUNDED SOULS

Healing Broken Boundaries

Dear Reader: In this chapter, I will not talk about sexual abuse, but I will speak about combating the lies we believe as a result.

Our South African home had two entrances. Formal acquaintances entered through the front door, which remained locked, while the rear entry had an unlocked metal gate. Friends and family knew to use the rear entrance rather than the front door, as it granted easy access into our home.

Sadly, people posing as family friends also gained entrance. When I tried to tell Mom what happened to me at the hands of one such poser, she minimized his actions—"Oh, that's just Bill." When Bill quickly figured out nobody would protect me; I endured years of hardship from him, as I had from many others. My escape came when my family packed our belongings into the cargo hold of a freight ship and sailed to America. While ten-year-old me was grateful to be moving miles away from harm, my secret burned in me for years.

Sadly, the gate to our home had been left unguarded in more ways than one, and destruction entered.

In an ideal world, parents establish healthy boundaries to protect their families instead of leaving the gate open for chaos to enter. Children are safeguarded and taught that no one has the right to bypass boundaries and harm them.

But what if our protectors abandoned their post?

Or worse, what if the parent is the abuser?

Perhaps, as a child, you tried to establish boundaries but faced protests like, "You're so private," "What's wrong with you?" "We are your parents," and so on.

These messages may have led to the mistaken belief that your body belongs to someone else. Furthermore, some victims believe they cannot disclose the abuse for fear of exposing the abuser. They have been manipulated into thinking they must protect the abuser's reputation.

I promised not to discuss sexual violations in this book, and I will keep that promise. However, the lies arising from such violations must be confronted.

The truth is that your body belongs to you.

There is nothing wrong with you for wanting to maintain that human right, nor for sharing your trauma with people who can help protect you.

Even as an adult, you do not have to sacrifice your body to please someone against your will. Abuse is completely abnormal. It must be healed through God's love in a safe community, as you learn to honor and safeguard yourself. Nobody has the right to pressure or coerce you into anything.

Your body is yours; as such, it is a gift to be given by you in a reciprocal, loving, covenant relationship. In 1 Corinthians 7:4—a verse some people misconstrue—we are encouraged toward mutual satisfaction, *never* dominance.

True love honors, doesn't push, and never violates. Wait for it; you deserve nothing less.

———————

Jesus compared His followers to sheep and Himself to both the shepherd *and* the gate of God's sheepfold. Because Jesus laid down His life on our behalf, we are blessed with complete access to God. That gate is always open to His sheep.

Jesus warned that anyone who enters the sheepfold by any other means is a thief and a robber (John 10). They bypass the gate. Trust me, when we are wounded and hurt, it is because people broke God's boundaries to do so.

Women, in particular, tend to feel that having boundaries is unbiblical. Many instances in the Bible disprove this; I'll provide one. In the Sermon on the Mount, found in Matthew 5, Jesus states that if a man even looks at a woman with lust in his heart, he has committed adultery. This protects both parties: the woman is shielded from the shame of violation, and the man is safeguarded from sin. Boundaries are profound and they are God's idea.

———————

A friend shared the details of her husband's betrayal. When she confronted him about his infidelity, he wept in despair and begged her to let him stay, promising to change. However, despite his promises, he maintained his addictive behaviors.

By the time we spoke, the cycle of abuse had undergone many iterations: She discovered his infidelity; he tearfully begged for forgiveness and promised to be faithful. They rebuilt a tenuous relationship, only for him to break trust again.

She wept as she recounted the toll it had taken on her, especially in concealing the truth from the community and their children. Maintaining the facade took everything she had.

We joined hands and prayed.

During prayer, I saw a picture of two backyards separated by a wooden fence. One yard was flooded, the other dry as a bone. Although both homes had running hoses, one had been flung into the neighbor's yard, causing the flood and contrasting desert. Neither yard received what it needed to maintain healthy growth. One got too much attention, and the other, none.

The flooded yard represented her husband. He had received more than enough attention from her and his lovers.

As we prayed, she recognized herself as the neglected yard due to prioritizing her spouse and overlooking her own needs for years. It was time to focus on *her* health. Helping him conceal his behavior from the community had only exacerbated the problem. The only healthy option forward was to liberate herself from his sinful cycle.

The fence represented a boundary that wasn't maintained in the marriage, with her hose watering his lawn. She understood that both individuals have personal responsibilities in a relationship. We cannot perform the other person's job for them; only they can do that. Her trust had been repeatedly violated by his failure to uphold his duties. *If* she chose to stay in the marriage, he must come clean and hold himself accountable daily to the community. She would need time and loving care from a support group, and they would both need counseling.

In the end, he chose his addiction and lost her. But she healed and walks in health and joy to this day.

Boundaries are not created *against* someone else; they

exist *for our* benefit. They are fluid and can be adjusted as necessary, *by us.* However, be prepared for potential backlash, as those who lack self-accountability typically resist boundaries.

I once dated someone who exhibited push-me, pull-me behavior. After a few enjoyable dates, he became fearful and withdrew without any communication, only to return later. He even claimed, "God told me I needed two weeks apart." If somebody tells you something like this, tell them to take as long as they like and not to expect you to be there when they come around. Sadly, however, I let this continue for nearly a year.

During our separations, he lived his life happily while I agonized over what I had done wrong. After his "divine" hiatuses, he returned as if nothing had happened. There's a saying that crazy people make you feel crazy. Indeed.

One day, I came to my senses. I told him if he wanted to reenter the relationship, he could do so as a friend—without kissing, handholding, or hugging. A clear boundary. Since he was in a pull-me phase, he agreed. And would you believe it? The same day, he reached out and took my hand. "I know you don't want anything physical," he said, "but I feel so close to you."

Typically, I would have minimized the indiscretion—*Who cares? He only held my hand. We've had a great day, so don't make a big deal of it,* and so on. But not this time. I wanted a relationship, but not on these terms.

"Actually," I said, "I told you I only wanted to be friends. If I can't trust you in a small area, I won't be able to trust you with things that matter. This ends today, whatever *this* is."

He stared at me, dumbfounded.

"I feel like someone just took away my favorite toy," he said in confusion. With that, he walked out the door, taking his drama with him. With his words, he perfectly summarized his toddler-like mentality. I'd been a toy to be discarded or played with at his whim.

In an instant, I realized I'd known this all along.

Moreover, the power to end the cycle had rested with me, but my fear of losing him kept me from ending things. When I finally mustered the courage, it felt so empowering; I wanted to shout it to the world! I went to the beach and ran up and down the shore, skipping in my newfound freedom. I had broken free from co-dependent thinking. I didn't need his approval to be okay. I was okay—more than okay—without him. I sensed God's pleasure in my healthy choice, the first of many to come.

Teaching from Titus 2:5, Devi taught a powerful truth about women as the keepers or guards of the home. She pointed out that God has given us spiritual authority to guard what we allow into and out of our homes.

Likewise, our bodies are God's dwelling. We have the authority to accept or decline what happens us. We are *more than justified* in saying no to those who seek to exploit our vulnerabilities; and to say yes to healthy, life-giving relationships. We may not have had strong gatekeepers in our youth, but it is not too late to stand tall for ourselves. We never have to compromise our values to please someone else. Those who say otherwise are unfit for a relationship.

There's a great story in the Bible about a Jewish man named Nehemiah. After the Babylonians plundered Jerusalem, they exiled many Jews and forced them into service. At the time of this account, Nehemiah served as cupbearer to King Artaxerxes. Constantly yearning for news of his homeland, he inquired of his friend Hanani about the Jews who had returned to Jerusalem after their captivity. To his distress, he learned that the walls of Jerusalem had been broken down, and the gates burned with fire. In a remarkable turn of events, he gained permission and funding from the king to rebuild them.

During the restoration process, Nehemiah rebuilt eleven gates. Each had a name, such as the Fish Gate, due to its proximity to a fish market, the Sheep Gate, and so on. In other words, each gate served a distinct purpose, made known by its title. Merchants and consumers passed through the gates, taking through what they desired to sell or bringing back what they had purchased. Every gate provided two-way access, except for the Dung Gate. The Dung Gate operated differently.

Dung went out, but new dung did not come in.

In your healing journey, many toxic memories will be expelled from your body as you work through the trauma of what you endured. I pray God heals you of every memory, as He continues to heal me of mine. But know this, you have the right to close the entrance gate inside of you, so to speak, to prevent unsafe individuals from bringing waste into your cherished soul. You are allowed to block unsafe individuals.

Dung should always go out. Never in.

During my journey, my mentors encouraged me to distance myself from my parents while I healed. Although it was extremely difficult for all of us, this separation allowed me to process my pain safely. I understood that I needed a boundary until they could acknowledge and stop justifying their wrongdoings. I emerged stronger and healthier.

There can be no true fellowship unless the people who wounded you repent of their behavior. If they continue to justify their abuse, they remain unsafe. The gate must close, even when it is heartbreaking to do so.

I have a favorite spot along a nearby trail. The crunchy gravel path dead-ends before an aqueduct. As the snow thaws atop the nearby Sierra Mountains, the runoff is channeled to our valley below, providing water for the fields. It's breathtaking to watch the emerald-green water as it tumbles powerfully over the stone walls. In the center of all this, a system of wheels and gates effectively manages the flow.

Without the boundaries of the aqueduct, the mountain water would never reach its destination. Similarly, without firm boundaries, God's precious and life-giving healing will not reach the depths of our hearts. Remember, a river without banks becomes a flood. Establishing walls around our healing journey protects and directs it for our benefit.

Spend time with Jesus. Ask Him to show you a safe place to process your pain. For me, it was professional counseling. God also provided two beloved mentors who faithfully took me under their wing for a few years. It is a gift I will never be able to repay; such is His mercy. Just as Jesus had an intentional path for me, He has one for you.

He promises that rivers of life will flow through Him to you. I pray the well within you—created through courageous boundaries—overflows with those waters.

CHAPTER 11

LESS THAN

Healing Perfection's Lie

At my doctor's recommendation, due to, and I quote, my "mature age," I purchased a gym membership to begin weight-bearing exercises.

After struggling to put on a pair of stretchy workout pants—actually, falling to the floor because my foot got stuck in the tight fabric of one leg—I tossed them into the donation pile and went shopping. With spandex-related items no longer an option, I tried on a pair of baggy parachute pants. I didn't injure myself in the process, and I even felt, dare I say it, cute.

The next day, I headed to the gym.

I hadn't been there long before a lady approached me. She said something, but I couldn't hear with my earbuds in. I took one out and leaned in to listen, my face a few inches from hers.

"Pardon me?" I asked.

"I like your pants," she said cheerfully.

"Thank you," I replied, smiling.

I'm not going to lie; I felt pretty good about myself for the remainder of the workout—I even wondered if other people liked my pants.

Before heading home, I washed my hands in the restroom. As I looked into the mirror, my mouth dropped. There was a blob of peanut butter from my morning breakfast smeared on my face. The same side where I had leaned into the woman.

Oh, but wait, that's not the worst of it. A chunk of a peanut was stuck to the creamy base. My mind reeled. I washed my hands and face and left the gym, shaking my head in embarrassment. Try as I may, perfection always lies just out of reach.

My sister and I used to devour books and magazines during our summer vacations. I'll never forget the mesmerizing article about a fictional girl named Jackie. *She* never left home with chipped nail polish or got fobbed off with a red sweater when she wanted green. My guess is she didn't attend events with breakfast on her face, either. She became our new catchphrase for people who appeared to have it all together. "I met a Jackie today," we'd say, going on to praise some merit or another.

I honestly don't know why we were so intrigued by this silly article. Perhaps our teenage brains enjoyed fantasizing about being admired. Perhaps Jackie represented calmness, when we lived in chaos. Nonetheless, this perfect woman became our unattainable brass ring.

Have you heard of the brass ring on old-timey carousels? A wooden arm is lowered randomly during the ride, dangling the shiny object. If a rider manages to grasp it, they win another go-round.

The only problem is that it's an illusion.

The ring is designed to remain slightly out of reach; when the horses go down, the ring goes up. Riders stretch their fingertips upward, while struggling to maintain balance, to win the elusive prize. Before they know it, the ride's over.

This raises a question. Why strive for another ride when the first one is so fraught with struggle? Why not just enjoy the first ride?

Similarly, the allure of perfection distracts us with unattainable things while robbing us of the joy of the present moment. We only get one ride through this wildly unpredictable and profound human life. What if we stopped striving for impossible standards and simply embraced our authentic, ever-evolving selves? Imagine if, regardless of all arguments to the contrary, we:

- Finished the book.
- Invited people to our messy house.
- Exited the toxic relationship.
- Took the meaningful job.
- Uploaded the inspiring post.
- Booked the adventurous trip.

There is so much life to be experienced, and perfection will never let us begin.

The illusion of perfection is an age-old lie. When God created Adam and Eve in His image, He placed them in a beautiful garden with fruit-bearing trees. They could eat from every tree except the tree of the knowledge of good and evil. If they ate of it, they would die. In this way, God gave His creation free will; they could choose obedience. Or not.

Seizing the opportunity, the devil tempted Eve to eat the forbidden fruit. In direct contradiction to God's warning, he said, "You will not surely die. For God knows that in the day you eat of it your eyes will be opened, and you will be like God, knowing good and evil" (Genesis 3:4-5).

Deceived, Eve gave the fruit to Adam, and they ate it. As foretold, death entered the garden. Although the devil's insidious temptation oozed with deceit, the core message was this:

You are deficient.

If you have felt inadequate in any way, it is rooted in the lie that you are not enough. Whereas God assures us *who we are* in Him, the devil masterfully conveys *who we are not*, manipulating our identity. He knows that if he can make us feel *less than*, we will search endlessly to fill the void with all his unholy remedies, never finding satisfaction.

Have you ever lamented, "If only I had this or that, my life would be complete," and then anxiously grasped at superficial things to fill the perceived void? I am not trying to cause shame; I have fallen prey to this lie many times.

I've passed up some object or other while shopping because it didn't feel like my style, only to later see it proudly displayed by an influencer as the "find of the century." Seeing how cute it looked in her home, I suddenly wanted it. I anxiously drove back to the store, hoping I hadn't missed what my life now desperately needed. I initially felt great about the purchase, but eventually, the object—which I never truly even desired at heart—lost its appeal.

Fear of lack creates the perception of a void.

When we try to fill this emptiness apart from God, it will only cause anxiety, hopelessness, and despair—that insidious brass ring promising everything and delivering nothing.

However, we can heal from the lie of perfection, it requires focus and trust.

———————

The truth is, Eve did not need another thing, yet the enemy convinced her so. His deception worked because he focused her attention on what she *didn't* have rather than what she *did* have. More is not better; it's just… more. How would you answer this fill-in-the-blank?

I need more _____.

I don't know what your thing is, but I do know this: unless you put Jesus's name in the space above, more of it won't fix your life. Trust me, I've tried. We must stop fixating on things God has purposely kept out of reach. But beware. The enemy makes what we shouldn't have more appealing than what we should and do have. Let's expose some of his schemes. Has someone else's home ever looked better than yours? How about their:

- Partner
- Car
- Friends
- Hair
- Family
- Vacations
- Jewelry
- Children
- Bible teaching style

The battle to turn away from the thing I anxiously desire, whether harmless or potentially disastrous, requires refocusing. Here are some practical habits I've found helpful:

- When I desire someone else's home, I clean mine. At the end, I light a candle and look around in satisfaction, realizing how fortunate I am to live here.
- When I desire a new item, I clear out a drawer to see how much stuff I already own. Often, I find I don't need more; I actually need less.
- When I'm tempted to compare myself to someone else, I practice gratitude or seek wisdom from a friend.

When struck by the "forbidden fruit of the moment," turning my gaze in these ways helps me refocus. Sometimes, however, the desire for something is so strong that it takes an even greater test of my will.

Years before I met and married Ted, my former husband left me. Although I didn't know it at the time, my lawyer later informed me that my ex-husband fully intended to divorce me and remarry. He began with a "trial" separation. As you can imagine, my emotions were bruised and tender. Coincidentally—or not—a very handsome man began to swing by my office in the mornings. He, too, was going through a separation. He rested his arms on the top of the door frame, his biceps bulging, and asked flirtatiously, "What's the Bible verse of the day, Andi?" Good heavens, how is anyone supposed to resist that?

It was my most significant Eve test to date. Would I reach for something not meant for me? I knew the door was open if I desired it.

I could almost hear the enemy's lies—*God is setting up your next husband. What are the odds of both of you going through a separation at the same time? This is God's provision for you.*

One evening after work, I left for home filled with angst. In a split-second decision, I drove my car past my exit and toward the mountains, pulling onto a deserted stretch of road. I got out, shut the door, and crawled onto the hood. Lying beneath the stars, I cried out to God. "You know my heart. You know I feel scared and abandoned. But I am going to fight for my marriage until the end. I've been faithful all these years, and I will continue to be faithful. Please help me. I give you everything, even if I end up alone."

In the stillness of the night, I knew what to do. The next day, I firmly told the man not to stop by my door again. Soon after, my then-husband left me for good. I moved to Southern California to attend seminary, where I met Ted. Three years later, we went on our first date, and six months later, we married, both of us crying with joy as I walked down the aisle.

What if I had given in to my desires all those years ago? I would have missed out on so much. In that moment of surrender, I refocused. I placed my trust in God, rather than in myself, embracing an uncertain future. It was a monumental moment of growth, shifting away from the fears of lack and loneliness that had driven me to my first faulty marriage.

The enemy separated Eve from God by sowing seeds of distrust, suggesting that God was withholding from her. Distrust leads to separation. Detached from God's truth, Eve became vulnerable to lies. She ate the forbidden fruit and ushered in sin and death. Then, in her fallen state, she attempted to hide from God among the trees, ashamed to see Him.

I've also been tempted to hide things from God because, honestly, I didn't want to give them up. Regarding one such habit, Jesus said with great compassion, "You don't have to give it up; just talk to me about it."

I never even regarded this as an option! In hindsight, confiding in Jesus about my temptation seems obvious. It felt so good to talk to Him about it. Jesus assured me He wouldn't withhold any good thing from me (Psalm 84:11).

Over time, through transparency and counseling, my trust wound healed. Realizing I no longer needed old habits to function, I willingly relinquished them. Your path may be different. Whatever your struggle, please don't let shame prevent you from asking Jesus for help. Invite Him into the process. As the source of every good gift, God will never hold out on you. He is generous; He is trustworthy.

It feels like the world incessantly nags us to up our game, whether it be buying a fancier home, getting a prettier haircut, sculpting a better body, or something else. We are bombarded with photos and posts on social media to feed our current obsession—convincing ourselves we are just gathering information or getting inspired. But here's the problem: without a strong sense of self, including what *we* like and who *we* are, we can get lost.

When my friend and I helped people style living spaces, most of our distress calls came from women who had spent a lot of money on furnishings. Upon arriving at the house, the frustrated homeowner would point to decorative online pictures, muttering how nice everything looked compared to her chaotic reality.

We always began by asking her what else she had, a counterintuitive question when piles of furniture surrounded us. She would reluctantly open closets in guest rooms or lead us to dusty garage corners. Shoved away from view, we often found an interesting vase, an old table, a funky painting, or something of that variety.

The homeowner often kept the object out of fondness but believed its old, shabby, or odd character made it unworthy of display. Despite her caution, we'd add the object to the mix.

When she saw its beauty through our eyes, the client would drag other things from closets, too.

The result was always a beautifully styled home, showcasing a blend of old and new that reflected the owner's true self.

Not perfect, but authentic.

———————

May I draw a tender comparison from this illustration to our lives?

Ashamed of past abuse or ongoing struggles that don't fit our desired self-image, we shove the broken, worn, and shabby parts of ourselves out of sight, especially from those who seem to have it all together.

Due to traumatic abuse, I believed my body belonged to whoever demanded it. I had a temper, felt entitled, made poor decisions, spoke disrespectfully to others, lied when frightened, and struggled with many internal emotions and external situations.

I yearned to fix my life but didn't know how. I practiced what I learned in childhood: to hide the messy parts and project a perfect image. I wish I had known then what I know now.

———————

We do not have to get our act together before coming to Jesus—He is the one who supports us and makes it possible.

Sinners, prostitutes, and tax collectors all flocked to Him and were mercifully received. He died on the cross, forgiving our sins and imparting His righteousness to us. Because of love's forgiveness and mercy, we can come as we are.

The fear that Jesus may ask you to relinquish a person, addiction, or lifestyle is a misplaced fear—do not let it keep you from approaching Him. Bring it with you. He will help you sort it out.

Will you stay as you are? Probably not. But do you truly want to? When Jesus transforms you into His image, you'll feel so free, you won't even miss the old version.

———————

Friends, perfection is a lie. *It promises everything and delivers nothing.* It is time to expose this lie and turn it upside down.

We are not deficient.
Perfection is.

Instead of pursuing perfection, pursue authenticity, peace, love, joy, friendship, humility, and transparency. In so doing, your life will become a beautiful, authentic representation of you—broken but forgiven, needing restoration but loved—perfectly imperfect.

Just like everyone else.

CHAPTER 12

DO YOU WANT TO BE WELL?

Healing from a Victim Mentality

I owned a Sheltie dog named Lily, who would leap high into the air and effortlessly catch tennis balls I threw. One day, while attempting to catch a ball, she yelped and fell to the ground. I rushed to pick her up, as she clearly could not walk.

A visit to our local clinic confirmed Lily had torn her ligament. Our veterinarian could not perform the necessary surgery, so we drove south two hours to the nearest facility. After a successful procedure, my dog emerged in a fluorescent pink cast, restricting her movements for healing. Six weeks later, upon its removal, she began to put tentative pressure on the leg.

A month or so later, due to the pressure Lily had placed on her healthy leg while the other was in a cast, that ligament also tore. We drove south for a second procedure, and after six more weeks, they removed the new cast. Lily healed, and life continued as usual—except, I noticed she still walked with a limp. I wanted her to have a healthy life, and these two costly surgeries should have ensured that.

I made an appointment at the surgery center to talk to the vet. As I sat anxiously in the waiting room, he emerged and asked to take my pup into the back room. "Alone," he added firmly.

Moments later, they returned. He held a ball in the air while she jumped, attempting to grab it from him. In what appeared to be nothing short of a miracle, Lily's leg had healed.

"What happened?" I asked incredulously.

He ignored my question. "May I ask what you do when she limps?"

"Well," I said, thinking carefully, "I hold her, massage her leg, and give her a treat. You know, all the normal things."

"Respectfully, Ma'am," he said, eyeing me closely, "you've trained your dog to limp."

The little rascal played me like a fiddle. You can bet all rewards for this nonsense stopped immediately. Soon enough, her leg and behavior straightened up.

There are many ways we may develop a limp in life. Sadly, numerous victims are trained—conditioned—by abusers to behave in undesired ways. This delicate area is best processed in a professional counseling setting, with individuals who can guide us through unlearning and undoing the destructive messages.

Limps can also develop simply through rewarding behaviors that keep us stuck in old patterns. You know the variety: *I had a bad day, so I deserve this wine, ice cream, chocolate, double-double from my favorite burger place, bag of chips,* or other indulgence. You'll never find me harshly disagreeing with this; bad days do sometimes deserve a treat. But when the sneaky treats forge even sneakier habits that cause us to limp, victim-like, through life—or worse, create debilitating addictions—it's time to address the root cause.

In his book *The Great Divorce*, C.S. Lewis says, "A wrong sum can be put right: but only by going back till you find the error and working it afresh from that point, never by simply going on. Evil can be undone, but it cannot 'develop' into good. Time does not heal it."

I have the privilege of mentoring women. It often takes time to mentally work their way back to where things went wrong. Sometimes, weeks of reflection turn into months; unraveling the past is a process. Lewis is correct, evil never turns into good. The terrible things that happened to you will never *ever* be okay. But when placed in God's hands, He can work them for good in our lives (Romans 8:28). I have lived this truth firsthand.

I had to learn that continuing to reward my wounds rather than addressing them only disabled me. While it felt easier, it wasn't making me well.

The Gospel of John tells of a man who, for thirty-eight long years, lay by the pool of Bethesda, whose stirring waters were believed to have healing properties. Many others lay there, but as Jesus walked by the pool with His disciples, He specifically asked this man, "Do you want to be made well?" (John 5:6).

You might think this a strange question. Obviously, someone who had lain on the ground for nearly forty years would *want* to be healed, right? The answer should be an instant, "Yes!"

The man, however, responds that he has nobody to put him into the pool, and even when he tries, another person gets there first. His response is lamentable yet understandable. He has been alone for decades, focused on the only solution he believes would change his circumstances: getting into the water. With great compassion, Jesus told him to pick up his mat and walk. Instantly, the man is healed. I believe that to shift perspective from victim to overcomer, we too must ponder Jesus's question.

Do you want to be well?

Before I began my healing journey, I responded similarly—*I don't have anyone to help me*. Previous abuse caused me to feel isolated and helpless. I often *wished* someone would carry me to the healing pool, that somebody would see my situation and fix it *for me*. To offer further transparency, I didn't want to face my past or do the hard work I knew lay ahead. I was afraid.

- Like the man, I did not say yes instantly.
- Like the man, I did not feel seen.
- Like the man, I did not count on the compassion of Christ.

Jesus turned me from the unattainable solution, always out of reach. He—*my solution*—stood right next to me, offering help. I wish our healing could be as instantaneous as it was for the man. It will not. Sadly, inner healing can often be a long and painful journey, but Jesus will walk with us. He is with us forever.

When I pray with people, I feel great compassion for their broken hearts. Sometimes, a person is not ready to begin their journey. I have learned to ask, "Do you want to be made well?" If they truthfully reply, "No," we pray for peace in God's timing. For those who are ready, we ask Jesus to show them how to begin.

To embark on our healing journey, we will need to use different and undeveloped muscles. No longer paralyzed, the man picked up his mat, representing his former lifestyle, and moved on. He exercised new muscles. He probably had to find a new livelihood, as he could no longer subsist on begging. And while I'm sure he was excited, his new job likely required a lot of hard work, doing things he had never done before.

Likewise, in shifting perspectives from *victim* to *victor*, we must leave behind old operating methods and learn new skills. While the result will be inconceivably meaningful, it will require hard work. I learned I needed to:

- Be respectful to people.
- Be teachable instead of defensive.
- Be kind, *all the time*, and never critical.
- Stop judging people.
- Be patient.
- Use my voice to benefit myself and others.
- Establish boundaries.
- Have more compassion.
- Give a genuine apology.
- Be gentler with my body.
- Stop people-pleasing.
- Become interdependent, not codependent.
- Listen to understand rather than make my point.
- Have more courage than I ever thought possible.

I didn't possess any of the skills listed above until I chose to change. I understood that nobody could do these things for me. I had to learn to do them. They were not easy to cultivate, and I continue to rely on God's grace every day. Sometimes I reflect on my previous behavior: defensive, disrespectful, and quick to anger. Thankfully, I've grown; I'm not that person anymore.

Do I still make mistakes and let myself and others down?

Of course! I'm human. However, the positive steps forward that I have taken with Jesus are with me forever. It is important to celebrate these milestones. And when, as I recently did, we inadvertently revert to old habits, these brief slip-ups only show how far we've come.

During a ski trip with my family, I arrived at the lift before they did. A man behind me, impatient for the next lift, hollered at me, "Move it!"—it seems like people behind me in line are always upset about something! Startled, I jumped out of line to accommodate him, but not quickly enough to avoid being hit by the metal chair lift. The force of the impact broke my knee. I think I'm the only person alive who has ever broken their knee while standing still.

I vowed never to ski again, but reluctantly gave in when my husband pleaded with me. Previously, I had been a good skier, handling difficult slopes with ease. Now, scared from my injury and long recovery, I insisted on only skiing the beginner hills.

The *whole* way up the mountain, I told anyone trapped on the chairlift with me about my injury. I went on and on about how scared I was to ski again—I did this all day long. By evening, so many people knew my tale of woe that no matter where I went, someone shouted, "Great job," or "You can do it!"

At one point, I even thought to myself, *For heaven's sake, Andi, stop talking about this!* But can you believe it? I didn't stop. My poor husband had to hear me tell the story over and over again.

The next day, I noticed Ted was a little grumpy. I went on a prayer walk and briefly mentioned it to God. In response, I heard, *What do you expect? You complained the whole day.* I laughed out loud, then went home to apologize. Yes, I had a traumatic injury, but did I need to process it ad nauseam? Definitely not.

At times, while still in victim mentality, I tried to process my trauma through others. I eventually learned it burdened them, even if they were kind about it, like the people on the slopes. Their compassion gave me some momentary relief, much like the treats I offered to Lily.

Nonetheless, it never fixed the root of my problem, it just reinforced unproductive habits. My pain was best processed in a safe and private place, with my willingness to change and grow.

It took time and deep self-reflection to form better habits and align my behavior with what Jesus desired of me.

In a well-known story from the Gospel of Luke, Lazarus's two sisters, Mary and Martha, invited Jesus to their home. Irritated by her sister's lack of help, Martha complained to Jesus. I love how free she felt to be herself in front of the Creator of the universe.

Instead of taking her side and telling Mary to help her sister, Jesus turned to Martha and lovingly instructed her, beginning with these words: "Martha, Martha, you..." (Luke 10:41). He told her that although she worried about many things, only one thing truly mattered: Him and His words.

Jesus didn't tell Martha she was unimportant. He simply shifted her focus away from her sister and worldly duties to more important things—the gift of His presence. To focus on Jesus, she needed to let go of her worries, release others from her expectations , and look to Him.

Martha, Martha, you.

In other words, examine yourself.

I used to sigh loudly while working around the house to guilt my husband as he rested on the couch after work. It never worked. Unbothered, he would literally fall asleep. I can laugh about it now, but back then I couldn't. I grew up in a chaotic environment, and my only sense of control was keeping my surroundings tidy. While tidiness still matters to me, it no longer drives me.

I learned to let things go, stop demanding others assist in performing my tasks, and ask for help in a non-passive-aggressive manner. Do I still get cranky when I trip over Ted's size-fifteen shoes, left next to the couch? Oh yes.

Progress. Not perfection.

And that's the way this victim-to-victor journey goes. We don't aim for perfection. We aim for progress. And little by little, we become so excited about living again, we can't be bothered to limp.

CHAPTER 13

MAKE A FAMILY

Healing Your Community

On the same flight that I battled an uncomfortable infection and asked the flight attendant for help, we landed too late in Vegas to make our connection to California.

The airline provided a free, courtesy hotel. But the second I saw the state of the filthy lobby, I knew there was no way I'd be staying there, not with my history of being taken to run-down hotel rooms by my abusers. I scrolled the internet for another place to stay while other displaced passengers from the same flight checked in at the hotel desk. Then, in a moment, everything changed.

I glanced up from my phone search. A young lady, about my daughter's age, waited in the queue behind me. When I saw her face, my troubles were forgotten.

"Hi, honey. Are you afraid?"

"Yes," she responded, tears threatening to fall.

"Well," I said, "see that big guy over there? That's my husband. You get a room next to us. I'll check behind the curtains and shower doors in your room, and we'll give you our phone number. If anyone messes with you, they'll need to mess with him first." Relief flooded her face. I looked around and noticed several other women, and introduced them to Ted, our newly elected security guard.

"Let's make a family," I told them. We huddled together, exchanged numbers, and ensured our rooms were close by. Trying to add levity, I sarcastically mentioned how happy I was to be in this hotel with the added bonus of an infection. We all laughed, and then one of the women asked if I happened to be part of a specific care facility in our hometown. When I said yes, she mentioned she worked there and would call in a prescription on my behalf. I couldn't believe the turn of events.

After we searched every lady's room for weirdos and found none, Ted and I went to bed—on top of the sheets with my coat on all night, I managed to get some sleep. The next day, as we boarded our plane to return home, I thanked the woman for her kindness to me.

"Well," she responded, "you're the one who made us a family."

I don't tell this story to brag about myself. I tell it for this reason: you may not have had a healthy family growing up, but you can make one anywhere.

Even in a scary hotel.

Finding your people and making a family is one of the most critical steps in your healing journey. And you have Jesus's permission to do so. He tells us in the Gospel of Luke that His family are people who do His will. If your parents abused you, that was not God's will. But you can find a new

Mom, a new Dad, and new brothers and sisters in Christ. That is God's will.

I'll never forget the first time I witnessed a loving church family. After many years of living in the United States, we returned to South Africa for a visit. Of course, every relative we'd left behind wanted to see us.

In particular, my wonderful aunt asked us to stay in her Johannesburg home. Waking up under the warmth of a duvet to the smell of tea and toast reminded me of the magical memories from childhood. It felt like a dream.

"Hello, my darling," she greeted me as I entered the kitchen, enfolding me warmly in a hug. So safe, so loved, I could weep just thinking about it.

While there, we attended her church. It had zero fanfare. After we sang a few worship songs, the pastor walked to the front and spread his notes on an old music stand. He announced the weekly potluck and reported about a person who had been in their prayers but had not yet turned a corner. Everyone murmured sadly. Some scribbled a reminder to pray. Then he gave his message, never raising his voice. Nearly forty years have passed since that Sunday morning, yet I still remember his talk about love.

That evening, we attended the "family" potluck meal. Everyone brought something and urged me, "Better try Aunty Aubrey's bread; it goes fast." People sat or stood in small groups to catch up on each other's lives. Nobody was left out. Prayer requests weren't gossip in disguise; these people genuinely loved one another.

That evening changed my life. I realized I needed a family.

My journey would have been vastly different if I had remained in my aunt's church group. I know with certainty I would have begun healing in the safe transparency they modeled. How could I not?

I wouldn't find a similar community until years later when I started my seminary studies. A lot had changed in me by then. I was even more broken and extremely guarded. My wounds ran deep, and I didn't trust anyone.

In one of my classes, a friendly man named Tim invited me to his home. "My wife and I host a group that meets every couple of weeks. Come on by. Nothing fancy, don't worry about bringing anything."

"Okay," I said, resolving to avoid him like the plague.

Tim continued to invite me for several weeks until, out of sheer embarrassment, I finally promised to come, silently vowing that my first visit would be my last.

When I arrived, his lovely wife greeted me. Their adorable daughter grabbed my hand and led me into her room to see her teddy bears and dolls. Dinner was some sort of crockpot meal —isn't it always?—followed by plenty of coffee and dessert. Afterward, in a flashback to South Africa, people shared prayer requests transparently. They asked after one another with such love and care; I was undone. To my shame, I started to cry. I had to leave the room. The girls followed me and put their arms around me. They didn't try to fix anything. They just sat with me as I let it all out.

Years of loneliness poured out as I released pent-up pain. After I finished crying, with a wad of Kleenex on my lap, I smiled at them. "Thank you."

"Of course," they replied kindly. And that was it. For the next three years, these were my people, my family.

In the Book of Acts, we learn that the early believers met "daily with one accord in the temple, and breaking bread from house to house, they ate their food with gladness and simplicity of heart, praising God and having favor with all the people" (Acts 2:46).

Simplicity of hearts. Nothing fancy, yet so valuable. They didn't just visit one another's homes.

They became one another's home.

They desired each other's company so much that they couldn't wait until the Sabbath. They met daily, searching with new eyes to find Jesus in the pages of scripture. This is what the body of Christ was meant to look like. We show up for each other and learn about Jesus.

We also know they had conflicts. A lot of Paul's letters address things that had gone awry. However, as they, as we, continue to grow, we will learn how to love one another—even through conflict.

I love good food. As much as I enjoy eating, I like preparing food for others even more. It's how I love people. I feed them.

Being raised in the South African culture of hospitality, we practically hound you to death when you're seated at our table, pressing you to accept seconds and thirds. My husband had to tell me gently that this can be considered impolite in the States. I'm still not very good at letting this custom go.

When Teddy and I started inviting friends into our home, we decided to begin each gathering around the table. We also established some ground rules, not to share with our people but to guide us as hosts. It was our way of ensuring an environment where our friends felt as safe as possible to receive love.

I hope you find them helpful for when you make your family.

- Have a start and end time, and try to stick to it. It's respectful.
- Host a meal. Ask people to contribute unless they cannot afford to.
- Take communion.
- Your house does not need to be immaculate, but it should be tidy.
- Worship Jesus. You don't need fancy equipment.
- Don't tolerate gossip or unkindness.
- Model loving behavior.
- Don't try to fix people.
- Pray for each other.
- Meditate on Scripture. Invite everyone to share and celebrate their insights.
- Text each other during the week.
- Love one another with all your heart.
- Let people go at their own pace, and release them with a blessing if they feel it's time to leave the group.
- Model humility.
- Have fun.
- And, as Larry Titus says, "Don't turn the lights off as soon as everyone leaves."

I think it's so much fun to make families wherever we go. Real families grow their connections and build the Kingdom of God. We are not out for ourselves. We look out for one another.

I had the opportunity to meet one of my heroes—Bob Goff. He has written several books on love and truly exemplifies his beliefs. I was thrilled to discover that he's every bit as genuine in person as he appears to be in public. I immediately noticed that he wasn't interested in keeping people at arm's length. He genuinely wanted everyone to feel special and to help them move toward their dreams. He reminds me of Jesus.

The Bible says Jesus is our brother. We are part of His family, and God is our Father. When we love people, we act like Him.

Surprise people with love.

Compliment people who look different from you, be interested in everyone, learn people's names, and love them. Be kind to your harried server in a restaurant, overtip them. More importantly, make a beautifully diverse family wherever you go.

I literally can't wait to meet you, dear sister or brother. While I can't promise not to ask if you'd like a second—or third—helping of food, I can promise to welcome you into my arms with a big hug. And, if needed, I can volunteer Ted to protect you against intruders.

After all, that's what families do.

PART FOUR

FIND MEANING
IN YOUR STORY

THE SUFFERING TREE

Healing Through Forgiveness

While visiting my sister in Michigan one winter, I walked through the woods near her home, crunching along deep snowdrifts. My breath appeared in frosty clouds.

I came across a seemingly ancient, barbed wire fence at the foot of her property and stopped to examine a giant oak that had fallen onto it. Instead of breaking the wire, the living tree had continued growing misshapenly over it, incorporating the barbed wire into its core.

Some people believe that suffering and grief naturally diminish over time: *as we grow, we'll forget.* But it's just not true. Suffering is more like the barbed wire, forever intertwined throughout the oak.

Look carefully at any tree stump, and you will notice rings in the trunk. Each ring represents a year in the tree's life. On closer examination—and if you know what to look for—you can find clues to what the tree went through during different periods.

Tight rings can indicate a challenging year of drought for the tree. Deprived of water, it didn't grow much that year.

Some rings bear proof of pestilence. Other rings are covered by ugly scars, marked from a lightning strike.

But this oak? It undoubtedly had barbed wire woven through numerous rings. The evidence of *years* of suffering remained within the tree. Remarkably, the tree continued to grow.

Likewise, we bear the evidence of suffering in our souls. But when we place our grief in the hands of Jesus, the gentle healer, we discover something profound. Not only do we continue to grow, we thrive.

> Our leaves provide shelter for others.
> The fruit of love is born through us.
> Strong and tall, we overcame the weeds that tried to strangle us.

Isaiah 53:3 prophesies about Jesus as "a man of sorrows acquainted with grief." Our Messiah suffered not for what *He* did but for what *we* did—and may still do. They nailed Him to the most significant tree of suffering that humanity will ever know. From this tree, He cried, "Father, forgive them, for they do not know what they do" (Luke 23:34).

Forgiveness and suffering have long been intertwined.

When we obey God's command to forgive and extend grace, we honor Jesus's great sacrifice. In such acts, we acknowledge the unfathomable mercy we received. As it cost Him to extend forgiveness, it will cost us.

Tim Keller said it best, "God's grace and forgiveness, while free to the recipient, are always costly for the giver.... From the earliest parts of the Bible, it was understood that God could not forgive without sacrifice. No one who is seriously wronged can 'just forgive' the perpetrator.... But when you forgive, that means you absorb the loss and the debt. You bear it yourself. All forgiveness, then, is costly."[1]

Keller is referencing passages such as Genesis 3. In the Garden of Eden, when Adam and Eve sinned, God established boundaries where none had been needed. He promised a Savior. Then, He sacrificed an animal to clothe them. An animal suffered that day to cover God's children.

Nearly four thousand years later, the promised Savior came. Jesus willingly suffered on the cross, and through His costly sacrifice, He forgave and covered God's children. To give eternal access to His Father, He absorbed all the debt we could not pay.

———

How, then, do we forgive? How do we extend the costly gift? Let me assure you, in case you've been told differently.

Not all at once.

Give yourself grace in entering the *process* of forgiveness. It begins the moment you bravely start your healing journey. It is an acknowledgment that you desire and deserve freedom—the wellspring of forgiveness. This grace is the end result of our healing journey, though present even in the beginning.

Holocaust survivor Corrie Ten Boom said, "To forgive is to set a prisoner free and discover the prisoner was you."[2] I did not know this quote over twenty years ago when my seminary professor assigned us to write a symbolic life journey, but it perfectly summarizes my depiction.

———

1   https://www.goodreads.com/quotes/260429-god-s-grace-and-forgiveness-while-free-to-the-recipient-are#:~:text=No%20one%20who%20is%20seriously,forgiveness%2C%20then%2C%20is%20costly.
2   https://www.goodreads.com/quotes/1283918-to-forgive-is-to-set-a-prisoner-free-and-discover

THE CAGE

An abused and frightened creature lay in a cage. She'd been trapped by people who hate animals. One day, Jesus opened the door, but the beast was too afraid to emerge. She would rather stay in the familiar prison, even though filled with fear and filth, than venture into the unknown.

Jesus was patient. He didn't pry her from the cage. He understood that even the rotting blanket upon which she lay was all she had and, therefore, dear to her.

After a while, He placed a bowl of warm milk outside the door. The creature warily lapped at a tiny bit and, fearing a trap, retreated to the deepest, darkest confines of the cage. Over time, she ventured to the bowl more frequently.

After a long while, Jesus gently extended His nail-scarred hand. The creature eyed it with caution yet felt intrigued. She understood scars, as she had them too.

In an act of love, she licked His wound, saddened that He had also suffered. She heard crying. She looked up and saw tears pouring down Jesus's face. Did He love her? Was He sad for her? He did, and He was.

He extended His arms. She stepped bravely into them, and Jesus pulled her close to His heart. There she remained, the two of them crying for wounds, for suffering, for the price of forgiveness.

As Corrie Ten Boom discovered, and I did, too, love and forgiveness set us free from prisons. And in our freedom, we release others. Once I healed, I no longer cared whether my abusers admitted their wrongs—were accountable to me. I knew God would deal with them because, through forgiveness, I had surrendered them to the righteous judge.

Jesus does not ask us to do anything He has not already

done. He gave us His Holy Spirit to provide us with all we need for the process of forgiveness.

––––––––––––

My mentors had a floral couch where I sat with my husband, Ted. He faithfully stayed by my side for two years, holding my hand as they guided me through my healing journey. By the end of our time together, even with eyes closed, I could accurately retrace every flower down to the leaf, petal, and stem, as I frequently looked down at the patterned couch to cry.

Gradually, I began to look up more with the support of their remarkable love. When Ted and I hugged them both goodbye on what we all knew would be our final session together, they put their arms around me and held me for a long while.

"Thank you," I said, through tears of gratitude. "I realized something the other day. You never told me to forgive."

"Of course not," the wife replied.

With her gracious permission, I now share my friend's reasoning with you.

"You were broken and shattered into many pieces. Our focus was completely on you. All your parts needed to heal—the abuse, neglect, nightmares, fears, how you felt about yourself, the pain in your chest, trips to the ER, and so much more. By being totally on your side and listening to you, we could wait for our precious Holy Spirit to lead us. As important as forgiveness is, that was not the time. It would have presented a roadblock. You were too fragile, your wounding too severe. As you became freer, you naturally assumed ownership of your forgiveness."

I recognized her wisdom. I could forgive only because they created room for healing. As I felt loved, I healed. As I healed, I forgave.

It is okay, more than okay, for forgiveness to take time.

Let me assure you of another truth about forgiveness. It does not require you to confront your abuser.

In her excellent chapter on forgiveness in *Longing to Belong*, a book I've mentioned previously, author Shawna Marie Bryant says:

> *Another misunderstanding about true forgiveness comes from the idea that we must confront the offender in order to forgive. According to the original Greek language, forgiving an offense sends away the negative effects and disregards the offender. You can forgive someone without ever seeing or speaking to that person again.*

This is crucial for survivors.

If you have been victimized, you never ever have to re-engage with that person or group again.

I have released many violent abusers who will never know so. Because of this, they no longer hold any power over me. I am in Jesus's arms—too busy being loved by Him to give them any more of myself.

Your healing, restoration, and forgiveness work can be done privately in the safety of your chosen community. *You can maintain this boundary for the rest of your life.*

Some may not have wounded you so intensely. In this case, you might wish to rekindle your relationship with them. This process, known as reconciliation, involves both parties engaging reciprocally and with immense patience. You may also need guidance from your community and possibly professional support to help maintain boundaries.

Ever since I recognized the dysfunction of my youth, I tried to reconcile with my parents but only received justifications in response. Justifications attempt to excuse the offender's actions. It says, "I did this because..." while repentance says, "I wounded you. I am sorry. How can I restore our relationship?"

Dad fully repented on his deathbed. We could have had a beautiful story had he done so sooner. My mom, still alive, chose to justify her neglect and bouts of rage as though a puppeteer had controlled her with strings.

Although I tried to help her understand the difference between justification and repentance, she was not willing. I forgave Mom, but, heartbroken, I ultimately had to let her go. You may wonder why I kept trying for so long. It is because I longed and prayed for reconciliation. She was praying too.

During a time when I had almost completely withdrawn, Mom called me by accident. Fortunately, when she noticed, she obeyed the Holy Spirit, who said, "Call her back." When I answered, she asked to discuss our relationship.

I reiterated my requirements for a genuine, reciprocal relationship. I reminded her that she was forgiven, but to remain in my life required repentance, not justification. Our relationship would remain superficial until she took responsibility for everything she had done.

She asked for an example. I explained how she had blamed my aunt for giving her bad advice on how to "silence" my panic attacks. I won't describe the details, but I developed claustrophobia from the abusive remedy. I clarified that it wasn't my aunt who had carried out the destructive advice. She, my mother, had. She must take responsibility for her actions and stop blaming others.

In a miraculous turn, she repented. "I own it all," she said. "What else do I need to own?" Shocked, I relayed only one more incident, as it covered the root of all others. She took *full* responsibility for her actions.

"I don't ever want to lose you," she cried.

I assured her, because of her actions that day, she had not. While I still uphold my healthy boundaries, our relationship changed for the better.

Forgiveness is a one-sided transaction. Reconciliation requires both parties' willing and humble participation. Although costly, it is powerful.

As a young child, I *never* thought I'd feel better.

I never pictured having a happy family of my own, with a loving husband and a beautiful daughter in a great community. Never could I have predicted laughter—the kind where you hold your sides, trying to breathe—because a friend said something silly. Nor could I have ever imagined the overwhelming joy of ordinary things, like drinking an espresso with a warm croissant, entirely at peace, once and for all.

I wish I could return and talk to that young girl. I would lovingly hold her hand and say to her:

Don't you worry about one thing. This pain you're feeling will turn into something completely remarkable. God, who calls you to heal, will heal you despite what happened. He will do it. Just trust Him.

You will never forget your suffering. Don't! That is how you honor your journey, yourself, and Jesus's healing work. The barbed wire will always be part of you, but not in the debilitating way you think it will. It will become a symbol of overcoming. Despite it, you will grow and bear fruit.

Keep growing, keep forgiving, and soon—oh so soon—your life will be almost too beautiful to behold.

CHAPTER 15

FOR THE SAVING OF MANY LIVES

Healing Your Legacy

When I was in second grade, our school in South Africa put on an end-of-the-year production for relatives and friends. Hundreds of community members filled the auditorium, eagerly anticipating the event, poised with flashbulb cameras; it was the seventies, after all.

Every year, tradition dictated that we reenact the same performance. The show never changed. Kindergartners wore cute rag-doll outfits and did a little dance, while third graders dressed in outfits resembling rain clouds and flowers. The rest of the grades had equally cute, fun costumes—fully dressed costumes.

But not the first graders. We were dressed like Hula dancers in grass skirts and a plastic lei. That was it.

No shirts, no coconuts, no nothing.

It should have been outlawed. I'll never forget how all of us girls cringed behind the curtains, dreading to perform our dance in front of the crowd. To our horror, our teacher urged us onto the stage as the sound of popping flashbulbs filled the air.

Whether we like it or not, each of us will be the recipient of tradition—a legacy—passed down to us. Some people receive godly traditions, inheriting love from parents who adored them and maintained a safe home. And others of us? Well, let's just say our traditions looked more like dancing half-naked on a stage. What I've learned in the end, though, is this:

Regardless of what happened to me, I can choose what happens through me.

Although I won't know for certain until I see him again in heaven, I believe my father will be proud that I have chosen to share the truth about our family's dark history. In his last moments, when Dad told me he didn't want to see Jesus without asking my forgiveness, he finally acknowledged that Jesus cared deeply about how he had treated me. He understood that the truth must come to light.

Just as the Olympic torch is kept ablaze as it is passed from one runner to the next, Dad's acknowledgment became the torch I picked up. I hope to spend the rest of my life using it to shed light for others trapped in darkness—to assure them that Jesus cares deeply about what happened to them.

I saved this chapter for last because, other than healing, I believe the most essential right for every survivor is our right to a legacy of love.

There's a great story in Genesis about Joseph, son of Jacob, and his remarkable journey from favored child to slave to ruler of Egypt.

Jacob's favoritism created hostility among Joseph's half-brothers, especially when he gifted Joseph a beautiful robe but did not do the same for them.

The hostility escalated when Joseph shared a dream revealed by God, in which his brothers bowed down to him. Despite their furious reaction, and in a serious lapse of judgment, Joseph chose to share another dream where the entire family bowed before him. Absolutely enraged, the brothers plotted his death and ultimately stripped him of his robe and sold him to a caravan of Ishmaelites bound for Egypt.

The brothers returned home, but, Joseph's trial had begun. After a horrific twenty-two-year ordeal, too lengthy to chronicle here, he eventually became a ruler in Egypt. During a famine, his brothers came to request food from the unrecognizable ruler, and ultimately bowed down before Joseph.

When Joseph revealed his identity to his brothers, he wept so loudly that the whole land learned of his distress. But here is the point.

When Joseph's brothers—rightly so—feared retribution, he assured them that they hadn't sent him to Egypt. God had. In so doing, Joseph took their perceived power over him from their hands and gave it to God.

Then, he comforted them with these words, "You intended to harm me, but God intended it for good to accomplish what is now being done, the saving of many lives" (Genesis 50:20, NIV).

After enduring twenty-two years of loss, separation, physical toil, and emotional pain, Joseph found meaning in his suffering. He understood it as the only way for a God-fearing young man to become the ruler of a godless nation.

Despite the harm his brothers brought upon him, he saw the greater purpose. God meant his terrible trial for good—to save many lives.

Will all of us touch as many lives as Joseph? Probably not. But can we impact more lives than we ever imagined? Resoundingly, yes.

Just as every pebble tossed into a pond creates a ripple effect beyond its initial impact, so too does our choice to heal.

When I chose healing, I valued myself.
When I valued myself, I chose a loving partner.
When I chose a loving partner, we created a loving family.
When we created a loving family, we forged a loving legacy.

I will not get to see how my choices transcend my lifetime, but I know this: My decision to heal has affected three people—my husband, my child, and me. While that may not seem like much, it's everything to me. I know how hard-won my victory is. And I'll be proud to tell my story to my heavenly Father when I meet Him face-to-face.

Although, I get the feeling He might already be aware and proud of me, too.

ABOUT THE AUTHOR

Andi Bull is a devoted Christian, wife, and mommy who enjoys spending time with her friends, family, and dogs— preferably at the beach with a cup of coffee. She lives in sunny California, loves bodysurfing, and store-bought cake because she is hopeless at baking. She has co-authored two books. This is her first independently written book.

A portion of the proceeds of this book will support anti-human trafficking efforts.

CONTACT

www.andibull.com

andibull@andibull.com

www.ingramcontent.com/pod-product-compliance
Lightning Source LLC
Chambersburg PA
CBHW031531120626
46545CB00005B/2099